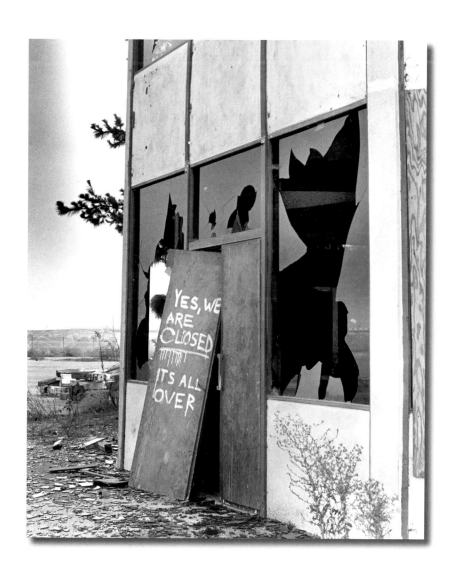

CarTech®

LOST
DRAG STRIPS
GHOSTS OF QUARTER-MILES PAST

TOMMY LEE BYRD

CarTech®

CarTech®, Inc.
39966 Grand Avenue
North Branch, MN 55056
Phone: 651-277-1200 or 800-551-4754
Fax: 651-277-1203
www.cartechbooks.com

Edit by Scott Parkhurst
Layout by Monica Seiberlich

ISBN 978-1-61325-045-7
Item No. CT514

Library of Congress Cataloging-in-Publication Data

Byrd, Tommy Lee.
  Lost drag strips : ghosts of quarter miles past / by Tommy Lee Byrd.
    p. cm.
  ISBN 978-1-61325-045-7
  1. Drag racing–History. 2. Racetracks (Automobile racing)–History.
I. Title.

GV1029.3.B97 2013
796.72–dc23

                    2012029954

Printed in China
10 9 8 7 6 5 4 3 2

Front Cover Photos

Top: In 1992, the tower still stood tall, and all of the track's bleachers and guard rails were still intact. At some point, the track was stripped and the buildings were torn down, leaving only the pavement to tell the story. (Photo Courtesy Mike Sopko)

Bottom Left: From the side of the Lions track, you can see the steepness of the spectator seating, as well as the minimal photographer's tower. "Big John" Mazmanian rips off the line in his well-known supercharged gas Willys coupe, which perfectly embodies the gasser styling we all know and love. (Photo Courtesy Don Gillespie Collection)

Bottom Right: Southern California was the ultimate drag racing hotspot, with several big-time tracks in the vicinity. Moving into the late 1960s, drag racing had evolved greatly thanks to a number of innovative gearheads. Mickey Thompson was one of the best, and this is one of his many drag cars doing its thing at Lions. (Photo Courtesy Don Gillespie Collection)

Title Page: Intense overgrowth has turned Hudson Drag Strip into a very eerie place. The bleachers are completely consumed by the trees and weeds; the pit side of the track is equally overgrown. However, the track surface appears to be in decent shape, as the concrete starting line was only a few years old at the time of closing.

Frontispiece: The crudely painted message on the door says it all. Even if you never set foot on the Orange County International Raceway property, this picture is a sad reminder that even the best drag strips couldn't survive the rapid urbanization of Southern California. By the mid 1980s, drag racing had hit an all-time low with multiple track closures. (Photo Courtesy Don Gillespie Collection)

Contents: A long expanse of asphalt is mighty tempting when you have two nostalgic vehicles lined up. The new owners are not welcoming to many visitors, but the right connections got these two ex-racers into the facility for a photo shoot. The vastly renovated Connecticut Dragway now features a number of test tracks for modern vehicles. (Photo Courtesy Trent Sherrill)

Foreword: Through the years, drag racing grew by leaps and bounds, with innovative drag cars being debuted at nearly every major event. In the end, the traditional single-engine dragster setup (such as this Ries/Chambers/Murphy example) topped all of the experimental builds until Don Garlits perfected the rear-engine design after his accident at Lions in 1970. (Photo Courtesy Don Gillespie Collection)

Back Cover Photo: You won't find a more classic drag racing photo than this one at Brainerd Optimist Drag Strip. It features a blown 1940 Ford Deluxe coupe squaring off against a 1932 Ford coupe with the flagman in mid-jump. After the drag racing scene dried up a bit, the 1932 Ford was sold off, where it went into hibernation for more than forty years. (Photo Courtesy Larry Rose Collection)

Author note: Many of the vintage photos in this book are of lower quality. They have been included because of their importance to telling the story.

OVERSEAS DISTRIBUTION BY:

PGUK
63 Hatton Garden
London EC1N 8LE, England
Phone: 020 7061 1980 • Fax: 020 7242 3725
www.pguk.co.uk

Renniks Publications Ltd.
3/37-39 Green Street
Banksmeadow, NSW 2109, Australia
Phone: 2 9695 7055 • Fax: 2 9695 7355
www.renniks.com

Contents

FOREWORD

I read the manuscript for *Lost Drag Strips,* and it brought back many memories—some good, some bad—as I had appeared and raced at almost all of the drag strips mentioned. I especially remember Lions Drag Strip, where I lost part of my right foot in 1970.

Tommy Lee Byrd has put a tremendous amount of effort into his research on the subject and I'm quite sure after he got into the project realized that he would never be able to cover all the abandoned drag strips located in North American. A few years ago I remember a couple of guys doing research on the subject and they worked on it for more than five years and were just really getting into just how many abandoned drag strips were out there.

Tommy Lee has touched on the most popular ones and you will find a lot of enjoyment in reading this book. I know I did, as I'm a history buff. I hope he does a sequel, because I think a lot of readers would enjoy hearing about the lesser-known abandoned drag strips around the country. Some of these little strips had a lot of exciting stories to tell. You would be surprised just how many of our Drag Racing Champions came from some small abandoned drag strip in a remote section of the country. The very first name that comes to mind is Shirley Muldowney, who did her first drag racing at Fonda Drag Strip in Upstate New York!

Don Garlits was a pioneer in the sport of drag racing, and he campaigned a fuel dragster for many years. This is the *Swamp Rat I,* and it was simple by design, but struck fear in the hearts of competitors. Garlits later ditched the multiple carburetors and went with a Roots blower and mechanical fuel injection. (Photo Courtesy Larry Rose Collection)

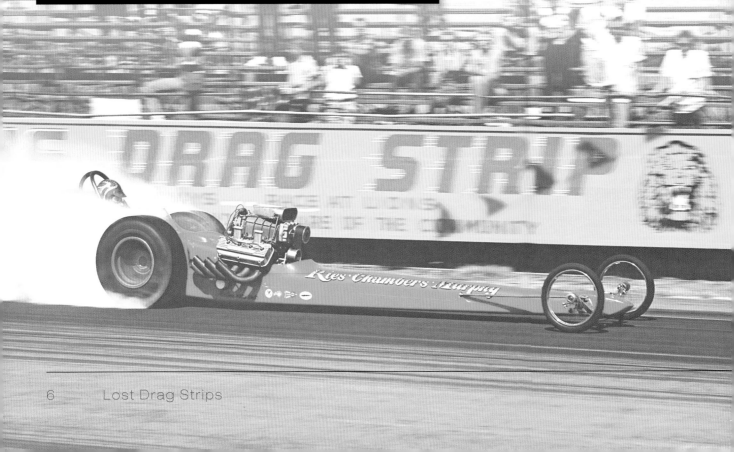

INTRODUCTION

There's no such thing as a forgotten race track. Someone, somewhere, has a memory from every motorsports facility that has opened its doors to the public at least once. Although this book focuses on drag strips, the same can be said for most competition venues in general. Unfortunately, because of my age, I don't have those great memories, but I plan to resurrect those good times within the pages of this book. I feature a great number of iconic tracks, showing photographs of each track's heyday, as well as photos of it in an abandoned state. There are also some tracks that may not be nationally known but hold a place in the hearts of the racers who called it their home track. Regardless of the size or the use of the track, you'll read about the history of each drag strip and learn more about the epidemic of closing tracks throughout the years.

There are hundreds of thousands of spectacular photos from many of the tracks featured in this book, but you've probably already seen them in other books, magazines, or maybe on the Internet. That's why *Lost Drag Strips* features never-before-seen photographs from private photo collections, provided by former racers, drag racing historians, and anywhere else I could dig them up. Some of the pictures have been used in other forms, but a great majority of the photos have been stored away in shoeboxes and photo albums for many decades. Prepare to see drag racing from a whole different perspective, from the landscape of the track, and the result of years of abandonment.

Some drag strips were immediately dismantled after closing, with the property being redeveloped into everything from basic neighborhoods to private airports to industrial

The heyday of drag racing turned average folks into car guys and it helped shape the automotive aftermarket industry. During the 1960s and early 1970s, the desire to go fast was no longer limited to the professional drag racing teams. It was an epidemic, and nitro-powered dragsters only fueled the fire. (Photo Courtesy Jay S. Magnum)

use. Others sat idle for years, allowing the structures and pavement to deteriorate. Either way the chips fell, it's sad to see such once-hallowed grounds in poor condition. The goal of this book is to rekindle the flame in the hearts of drag racers and spectators who experienced good (or bad) times at any of the tracks featured.

The first two chapters are an overview of the rise and fall of drag racing, in regard to the number of drag strips in operation. You'll learn why particular tracks closed, and get some details about a few of the very serious accidents that forced tracks to conform to new regulations.

In Chapter 3 through Chapter 6, you see before and after photos of drag strips in the Western, Midwestern, Northeastern, and Southern regions of the United States. They are a step back in time and a look at the tracks' current condition.

Chapter 7 focuses on the drag racing hotspot of Chattanooga, Tennessee, one of many during the 1960s. See before and after photos from drag strips that once resided within 100 miles of Chattanooga, with only a handful still in operation.

Chapter 8 features a few tracks that have received a second lease on life, with miraculous comeback stories, which are certainly rare cases in the world of drag racing.

These days it's still common for drag strips to cease operations and close the doors for good. Disagreements with local government officials rank high on the list of reasons for drag strip closure, but sometimes, a landowner simply gives up on it. While some tracks had a definite reason for closing, others ground to a halt due to a lack of support from racers. The sad truth is that many drag strip closings could be prevented, but the hobby has downsized since the heyday, so some tracks have little choice. Some might say that the sport of drag racing is bigger than ever, with million-dollar sponsorships and national television coverage, but I politely disagree. Gone are the glory days of drag racing, when grassroots innovation and

Some drag strips (such as 411 Dragway in Seymour, Tennessee) took on the appearance of an abandoned track long before closing the doors. A general lack of maintenance spells disaster for most racing facilities. When racers stop showing up, spectator counts dwindle, which creates a vicious cycle that never ends well.

The harsh reality of the modern era of drag racing is there are hundreds of abandoned race tracks in the United States such as this one (Hudson Drag Strip in Hudson, North Carolina). Some of them were well-known tracks that made a huge impact on the sport; many of them were hometown tracks that offered consistent weekly racing programs for many years.

Finding abandoned drag strips can be tough, but road names can sometimes provide the necessary hint. If you know a particular town had a drag strip, but you can't seem to figure out where it was located, it doesn't hurt to search for a county road that has "drag strip" in the name.

dare-devilish drivers ruled the quarter mile, and did it simply for the love of the hobby.

It's not all doom and gloom though; new facilities such as Z-Max Dragway in Charlotte, North Carolina, are paving the way for future super tracks, while revamped facilities provide hope for smaller tracks across the country. In most parts of the United States, you can easily travel to a drag strip and enjoy great, side-by-side racing every weekend during the racing season. With hundreds of tracks being abandoned over the past fifty years or so, it might take a little more driving than before, but if you're dedicated, you can make it happen. Support your local track and keep it alive, so if there happens to be a sequel to this book, your home track will stay clear of it!

Looking back on the glory days of drag racing, it's easy to see where the hobby got its roots, even though modern-day drag racing is so far away from its earliest beginnings. These days, drag racing is a highbrow business, with big-money sponsorships, high-tech equipment, and tow rigs that require a commercial drivers license. If any of those three items gets your gearhead juices flowing, more power to you, but I enjoy stepping back to a much simpler time in the sport—when crude cars and ruthless drivers made it exciting to watch, as each racer used unorthodox ways of finding speed. This type of innovation led to many breakthroughs in the drag racing industry, but our story starts in the late 1940s, when drag racing had no industry, and racers had no ulterior motives, besides going faster than the guy in the other lane.

Although the thought of racing two cars in a straight line had occurred to many people before World War II, this form of racing definitely saw a huge boom in popularity in the late 1940s, when an influx of mechanically minded men returned from the war. This was also the beginning of hot rodding in general, which completely changed the scope of being a car guy. Before this time in automotive history, if you were interested in modified cars, your attention was

By the end of the 1940s, the exhibition of speed was nothing new but it certainly increased in popularity. As seen in this photo from Daytona Beach, Florida, this 1934 Ford sedan ran a NASCAR-sanctioned 100.92 mph in a one-mile run. That's a strong number for the time, from what looks to be a street car. (Photo Courtesy Larry Rose Collection)

As the years passed, engine swaps, extensive chassis modifications, and experimental drivetrain combinations made for some very unique cars. At Maryville Drag Strip in Tennessee, this '32 Ford five-window coupe looks to be mostly stock, with power from a 348-ci Chevy W engine. For a very short window of time (1958–1965), the W engine was a phenomenal powerplant for race cars across the country. (Photo Courtesy David Giles Collection)

Drag racers only needed a strip of pavement to have some fun, but the development of timing systems helped the hobby become a legitimate motorsport. Sometimes drivers raced as far as the track allowed (sometimes upward of a half mile) but a quarter mile eventually became the standard length for the timed portion of a drag strip. (Photo Courtesy Larry Rose Collection)

Safety-Minded Hot Rod Club Plans 'Drag Strip' To Lure 'Speed Urge' Off Crowded Highways

'Roadmasters' Invite Judge to Be Member

By JULIUS PARKER

A hot-rod club, which places so much emphasis on safety that it wants to make City Traffic Judge Riley Graham an honorary member, last night mapped plans for acquiring a suitable drag strip in or near Chattanooga.

The organization, the Roadmasters' Club, probably has the "coolest drivers" in town.

It is composed of teen-agers, young men and several young-at-hearts who have more than the average share of gasoline mixed in their blood stream. Some of the budding mechanical geniuses have built and are building their own engines and hot rods.

They met last night at the Brainerd branch of the Hamilton National Bank. Meeting with them by invitation were Dr. William G. Stephenson, Asst. Atty. Gen. Henry Grady and several other advisers.

'SPEED URGE'

Charlie Epperson, president of the newly-formed group, explained it like this:

"There is a speed urge in most young people and a lot of older people for that matter. This leads to drag races down our crowded and narrow highways—a very foolhardy sort of thing.

"Our organization wants supervised drag racing. A drag strip is the only way of getting the speed urge off the highway and onto a properly supervised strip."

Although essentially a hot rod organizatoin, which expects to be sanctioned by the National Hot Rod Organization, Epperson

(Continued on Page 9, Column 3)

BIG WHEELS OF ROADMASTERS' CLUB—Shown above are officers and an adviser of the newly formed Roadmasters' Club, a hot rod organization dedicated to safety as well as speed. Seated, left to right, are Charlie Epperson, president, and David Prater, vice president. Standing, are Johnny Morris, secretary; Dr. William G. Stephenson, an adviser, and Buddy Houts, treasurer.—(Staff photo by Delmont Wilson.)

When the drag racing bug spread, cities and towns across the country felt the negative effects of street racing. During the 1950s, many car clubs inspired the construction of drag strips, such as the Roadmasters Club, which helped form the first Brainerd Optimist Club Drag Strip in Hixson, Tennessee. (Photo Courtesy Larry Rose Collection)

Wally Parks is responsible for legitimizing drag racing, mainly for his hard work in developing the National Hot Rod Association (NHRA) in 1951. More than fifty years later, the rulebooks have been re-written many times over, but Mr. Parks certainly laid the ground work for one of the most popular motorsports.

more than likely geared toward Indy car racing, which was the only prominent motorsport, aside from salt-flat racing, which started in the 1930s.

Indy car racing was not suited to grassroots car guys, as it required big-time money to keep up with the competition. To this day, Indy car racing is still a high-tech motorsport that limits the number of racers by pricing the majority of them out of competition. The initial concept of drag racing made it easy for the average guy to compete with like-minded individuals, without requiring a heavy engineering background and a ton of money.

With no place to legitimately compete, early drag racers used any straight, flat surface to line up and put the hammer down. Unquestionably dangerous for both drivers and on-lookers, drag racing was regarded as illegal soon after its inception. This pushed folks to find a safer place to race, and what could be more perfect than an airport? Long, straight, and flat, airport runways served as drag strips for quite some time, but as the hobby grew, so did the need for legitimate racing in a safe, yet exciting environment.

The first purpose-built drag strip was in Southern California, and is known as the Santa Ana Drags. It began operation in 1950 on an airstrip, and it gained the attention of salt-flat racers because of its revolutionary timing system. At the time, salt-flat racers wanted all-out speed, rather than a timed affair recorded at a particular distance, so it took some adjustment for the salt-flat guys to get the hang of the shorter race distances. There were no regulations, in terms of racing distance, but through the years, the quarter mile ended up being the distance of choice. Unfortunately, many quarter-mile tracks suffered from crashes and near misses due to dangerously short shutdown areas, so many of them were shortened to an eighth mile during the 1970s and 1980s.

Regardless of the danger, or your preference for eigth-over quarter-mile tracks, drag racing is still a popular pastime, and much of its success can be credited to one individual—Wally Parks.

Wally Parks was an instrumental part of the hot rodding and drag racing industry, having helped found the Southern California Timing Association (SCTA) in 1947, as well as the National Hot Rod Association (NHRA) in 1951. Things moved quickly as the NHRA assembled rules, classes, and organized races by 1953, and held its first official race at the Los Angeles County Fairgrounds, in Pomona, California. Although the racing surface for this event was essentially a parking lot, the NHRA gathered quite a following before it blossomed into the multi-million-dollar operation it is today. If not for Parks and several other influential car guys, the sport may not have gone mainstream at the right time, which would leave me with little to write about in this book.

During the 1950s, most parts of the country still used airport runways as drag strips, but the West Coast ways soon moved across the country, with drag strips popping up everywhere. From big cities to small towns, drag strips became more common. Compared to other forms of racing, drag strips were fairly simple to build, especially in the early days. If you had a strip of pavement wide enough for two cars, and a way of telling who won the race, you were in business. Find a place for people to park, give them a good vantage point to watch the racing, and you had a world-class facility. Safety wasn't a huge concern in the beginning, so guardrails or concrete barriers weren't common.

Regardless of geographic hurdles, drag strips were constructed across the United States as early as the 1950s. Many tracks on the East Coast had uphill shutdown areas. This elevation change helped bring the cars to a halt. This is a classic shot from Pittsburgh International Dragway. (Photo Courtesy Bill Truby)

As you can see from this mid-1950s photo, there was no Christmas tree, no guardrails, and no fear. Innovative by nature, these early dragsters were experimental machines, making the level of danger extremely high for drivers, track crew, and spectators. This dragster smokes what is undoubtedly a pair of re-capped slicks. (Photo Courtesy Larry Rose Collection)

Technical inspection was also lacking, but the NHRA made this a mandatory process in order to compete in one of its events. This changed the sport drastically, although outlaw tracks still had the "anything goes" mindset, which offered its own level of excitement. In 1955, the NHRA held its first national event, which drew an unbelievable crowd of racers and spectators to a drag strip in Great Bend, Kansas. Attracting more than 200 cars and 15,000 spectators in this first-of-its-kind event, the NHRA knew this was the way to really make money and take drag racing to the next level.

"The Nationals" then traveled to various drag strips around the country before arriving at its final destination of Indianapolis, Indiana, in 1961. And while big-buck tracks held NHRA events in the late 1950s, the small-town tracks were slow to evolve, but still managed to draw enormous crowds with high-stakes match races, and lots of interesting grassroots racing classes.

Many of the early tracks simply lacked the equipment necessary to hold a major event; some even lacked pavement. How can you have a drag strip without pavement, you ask? Packed dirt or clay seemed to be the answer for quite a few Southern tracks. A concrete or asphalt launch pad was generally only 100 feet in length, and then the track was dirt the rest of the way. If you wanted wild action and a huge element of danger, dirt drag racing was the answer because traction was nonexistent. Many of these drag strips were later fully paved and campaigned as a regular quarter-mile drag strip.

Back then, it was extremely rare to see a track owner intentionally build a track shorter than a quarter mile, even though eighth-mile tracks are so popular these days. In the

Small town guys, especially those in the East, didn't always have the budget for a fully paved drag strip, so dirt drag strips were fairly common, such as this one at Dalton Drag Strip in Maryville, Tennessee. Most of the time, these dirt tracks had a concrete or asphalt launch area (no more than 100 feet), with the remainder of the track being a hard-packed dirt or road-base mud/gravel material. (Photo Courtesy Larry Rose Collection)

It didn't take long for ingenuity from diehard drag racers to kick in, as evidenced by this 1932 Ford coupe fit with a Roots-blown Hemi in the very early 1960s. Whitewall slicks, disc hubcaps, and a custom interior gave this Deuce coupe plenty of style, and you can bet it was wickedly fast. (Photo Courtesy Larry Rose Collection)

The action in this photo took place at Paradise Drag Strip in Calhoun, Georgia. It is still active.

There was generally no option when it came to the budget of your build. Drag racers didn't purposefully build a low-budget car—it just happened. This dragster is a home-built piece. The fellow in the sunglasses is Jim Smith of Dayton, Tennessee. He built, tuned, and drove the Hemi-powered rail.

Ramp trucks were very common forms of transporting drag cars in the 1960s, as were regular passenger cars with custom dragster trailers. It was generally assumed that low-budget racers flat-towed their race cars to the track, while the "big-money" teams used car haulers and trailers. (Photo Courtesy Norbert Locke)

ate 1950s and early 1960s, some tracks were a fifth mile (1,056 feet) in length, while some others restricted certain classes to shorter distances than the full quarter mile. This approach is similar to the modern era, where the NHRA has limited its nitromethane-fueled classes to 1,000 feet instead of the full 1,320 to limit top speeds and hopefully improve safety.

In prior years, when races were generally held on abandoned airfields, the length of the track was not an issue, but short shutdown areas were quite common with purpose-built drag strips. Racers simply had to figure out ways of making their vehicles slow down quickly, so military parachutes became supplemental braking power for the faster cars of the 1950s. Drag racers still use parachutes today, but companies such as Simpson Performance Products and Deist Safety make them specifically for drag racing, instead of the old ring-slot design, which was known to create too much drag. So much, in fact, that it caused the cars to come off the ground momentarily. It also created health concerns with the amount of negative g-force applied to the drivers.

Again, in the early days of drag racing, it was all about trial and error, and it evolved into a legitimate motorsport while racers still continued to experiment with outlandish concepts. These days, it's not often you see a truly innovative drag car, but in the golden era of drag racing, crazy ideas were put into motion, and soon, racers were trapping speeds close to 200 mph in home-built dragsters. During this time, drag racing was still a grassroots motorsport, and you didn't have to have an 18-wheeler with living quarters and a double-stacker trailer to go drag racing. In fact, you were considered "big money" if you hauled your car to the track on a ramp truck or a trailer. Most cars were flat-towed in the early days, right into the 1960s.

The Cars

As racers desperately tried to increase speed, weight reduction became the focus as a way to go faster without spending money. This encouraged racers to strip down their

It's hard to deny the creativity used in drag racing during the 1950s and 1960s. This wild dragster was built and raced by Red Stanley. It is a prime example of ingenuity, with its heavily drilled front axle, aerodynamic inner and outer wheel discs, and an interesting engine setup with six carburetors. (Photo Courtesy Larry Rose Collection)

Inadequate traction and the lack of today's safety standards made for some interesting creations from car guys of the 1950s. With every race being a learning experience, the cars and drivers gained speed nearly every time they hit the track, even with limited resources for speed parts. This photo was captured at Brainerd Optimist Drag Strip in Hixson, Tennessee. (Photo Courtesy Larry Rose Collection)

cars—something that had already been seen in the salt-flat racing world. Low-slung roadsters and stripped-down coupes made up the majority of race cars, but more serious racers realized moving the entire engine toward the rear increased traction by greatly changing the car's front-to-rear weight distribution. Eventually, this mindset led to what we now call a dragster.

Although racers first used original factory-made frame rails to build dragsters, custom-built round-tube frames reduced weight even further and allowed for any engine and drivetrain combination imaginable. There is no question that racers' imaginations were much more vivid in the early days of drag racing. With no regard to their own safety, drivers threw tons of power at home-built cars, and didn't complain to the track owner if the track didn't hold it. They drove those cars like madmen and it added fuel to the already uncontrollable drag racing fire in the hearts of car guys across the United States.

Whether you raced a basically stock passenger car or a cobbled-together dragster, the late 1950s saw a number of breakthroughs in the sport of drag racing. Influential car guys developed components to increase speed, using many different mindsets. Marvin Rifchin was one of those guys, and he is responsible for producing the first drag racing slick in 1957. At that point, M&H Racemaster had actually been around for a few years, but Marvin concentrated on circle track racing before jumping into the drag racing world. Before the introduction of M&H slicks, racers used recapped tires, which provided marginal traction and a high failure rate at extreme speeds.

When a young man by the name of Don Garlits used a set of M&H slicks to win a big race in South Carolina, the other racers took notice, and the drag tire industry began. The same story can be told for many innovative products in the drag racing realm, but tires have always been a big deal, in combination with a good-working track.

Throughout the 1960s, the number of drag strips continued to increase. Many racers were able to quit their day jobs and race professionally, although it certainly didn't make anyone rich in the beginning. Relentless traveling from coast to coast resulted in tired eyes and sore backsides, but the thrill of competing against the nation's best racers made it worth the effort.

As racing caught on, and racers found new ways of going faster, dividing the vehicles into respective classes leveled the playing field. Restrictions in regard to vehicle weight, engine

The famed *Speed Sport Roadster* was an innovative machine with its mid-engine design and nitro-swilling Hemi, and it's one of the most recognizable drag cars from the late 1950s. You can tell this is a later photograph of the car because the "Speed Sport" lettering has been changed to "Howard-Weiand Equipped." (Photo Courtesy Larry Rose Collection)

By the mid 1950s, drag racers were desperate for traction, which influenced the development of purpose-built racing tires. Marvin Rifchin manufactured the first slick in 1957, and set the drag racing world on its ear with mind-blowing improvements in elapsed times and speeds. These 7.60-15 M&H Racemaster tires are mounted to a pair of Romeo Palamides magnesium wheels.

cubic inches, and many other parameters made the classes distinct, but many tracks used different sanctioning bodies with varying rulebooks. With the rapid growth of the sport, class rules changed often, and almost every car in competition was a record holder at some point due to the many sanctioning bodies, racing classes, and rule loopholes.

By the mid 1960s you could compete professionally in the NHRA, the AHRA (American Hot Rod Association), or countless independently promoted events and match races. Just because a racing organization didn't have a fancy, four-letter acronym didn't lessen its importance in the racers' eyes, so a great number of small tracks attracted very well known racers to their facilities by offering big purses and even bigger bragging rights.

It was hard to deny the popularity of drag racing, especially when race tracks kept popping up across the country throughout the 1960s. Before that, folks were desperate for a place to race, and the influx of tracks resulted in a number of drag strip choices in many areas. Many tracks joined forces in the 1960s to co-promote local points series, where racers competed at one track Friday night, moved to another track on Saturday, and then another on Sunday afternoon. This three-day attack made for great racing, and many tracks were in close enough proximity for spectators to view all three events, so it was a win-win for racers, track owners, and spectators.

And while big-time West Coast tracks such as Lions Associated Drag Strip and Riverside International Raceway provided Top Fuel racing on a regular basis, the smaller tracks offered wild action with an outlaw atmosphere that kept gearheads coming back every week. This outlaw attitude was highly evident in the South, and it still lives on many of the remaining tracks.

During the 1950s, drag strips drew enormous crowds, even to the smaller tracks that never stood a chance of holding a national event. This photo was taken at Brainerd Optimist Club's first drag strip in Hixson, Tennessee. More than 5,000 spectators entered the track on its opening day. (Photo Courtesy Larry Rose Collection)

Dragsters

Top Fuel dragsters were hot at the big-time tracks on the West Coast and racers across the country worked hard to keep up with the big guns. In the early days, dragsters were very basic racing machines, built primarily from two frame rails, an engine, and a place for the driver to sit. Very light in weight, dragsters were the ultimate drag racing machines, and it didn't take long for racers to come up with new ways to go faster. The formula was simple, but the lack of legitimate speed parts limited horsepower for a while.

This is a great example of drag strips working together to organize an incredible event, which took place at three different tracks on three consecutive days. The "World Series" drew many Super Stock cars and created a huge buzz in the three towns, making for an unforgettable three-day series. (Photo Courtesy Richard McFalls)

Dragsters definitely put on a show during the 1960s. With the chest-thumping exhaust note of a nitro-injected engine and the watering eyes that accompanied it, these beasts have always been extremely popular. During the early days dragsters were push-started and then blasted off the line, leaving behind a trail of tire smoke. It was a beautiful sight. (Photo Courtesy Don Gillespie Collection)

As dragsters evolved during the late 1950s, there was no end in sight. From 1960 to 1970, you could count on Top Fuel cars to literally grow 10 inches in length every year, making the cars more and more stable at high speeds. Various front axle and suspension systems passed through the experimentation process, from solid-mounted axles to transverse leaf springs to torsion bars. The rear suspension was never a factor, as it always remained solid-mounted.

Unlike today's top classes, the engine setups were very diverse as experimentation took a firm grasp on the sport.

Multiple engines were a popular trend for a while, but the single-engine dragsters were nothing short of extraordinary. Back then, there was no such thing as a cookie-cutter engine, because Pontiac, Oldsmobile, Buick, and Cadillac engines were all part of the game, even among Chevy, Ford, and Mopar offerings. Even within the big three, there were a number of choices in potent powerplants. Chevy had the tried-and-true small-block and then the big-block in 1965, while Ford had the 427-ci SOHC engine, and Mopar had the Max Wedge and then the Hemi.

Experimental supercharger setups, advances in fuel injection technology, and revolutionary ways of transferring power to the rear end kept the hobby interesting for quite some time. Racers learned something new at every race, and generally made vast improvements with little planning—try something different and see if it works. The sport's most influential trendsetters, such as Mickey Thompson, Joe Mondello, and Don Garlits, set the standard, but it didn't take a big name to make long strides, in terms of speed.

Dragsters remained in the front-engine configuration until Don Garlits' unfortunate accident at Lions Associated Drag Strip in Wilmington, California. The event happened in 1970, and Garlits was out of commission until the next season,

Don Garlits was a pioneer in the sport of drag racing, and he campaigned a fuel dragster for many years. This is the *Swamp Rat I,* and it was simple by design, but struck fear in the hearts of competitors. Garlits later ditched the multiple carburetors and went with a Roots blower and mechanical fuel injection. (Photo Courtesy Larry Rose Collection)

When the NHRA put a ban on nitro in 1957, drag racers had to find other ways of making power, so many resorted to superchargers. Generally, these blowers mounted atop the engine, but many racers used a Potvin blower drive, which positioned the blower in front of the engine (driven directly off the crankshaft) for better aerodynamics and driver visibility. (Photo Courtesy Larry Rose Collection)

Front-engined dragsters were common for many classes, even after they were phased out of the professional ranks. This example raced at Motion Raceway in Assumption, Illinois. (Photo Courtesy David Giles Collection)

After Don Garlits' horrific clutch explosion at Lions in 1970, he set out on a mission to build a successful rear-engine dragster. Many had been constructed, but none of them had the success of the standard front-engine cars. By the late 1970s and early 1980s, the rear-engine design was a tried-and-true design with many safety features. (Photo Courtesy Don Gillespie Collection)

but he debuted a new design that set the drag racing world on its ear—a rear-engine dragster. Keep in mind that rear-engine cars had been built before, but the design was never perfected until Garlits introduced the *Swamp Rat XIV*.

This new design made for a quick transition into the professional fuel ranks, but many of the slower classes kept the front-engine configuration for several more years. Then front-engine dragsters began to be phased out, and many of them were scrapped because no one wanted an outdated race car. Imagine everyone's surprise a few decades later when nostalgia drag racing hit an all-time high, and those vintage race cars became priceless pieces of history. The ones that survived are certainly highly coveted artifacts.

Super Stock

Although Top Fuelers were high-tech considering the era and drew huge crowds of spectators, another series of classes formed to cater to the grassroots guys. It was called Super Stock and it evolved from the many levels of stock-class racing.

Super Stock racing got its start in the early 1960s, when many American automobile manufacturers began producing high-horsepower cars from the factory. Big cubic inches, multiple carburetors, and increasing compression ratios quickly turned into 400-hp production cars. Chevy had the 409-ci W engine and Ford had the FE-based big-block, while Mopar had the Max Wedge and Hemi. In an effort to keep pace, other makes had unique offerings too, such as the Pontiac Super Duty 421.

The idea of the class was to limit the output of the cars by putting restrictions on the engine modifications. No power adders are allowed in Super Stock to this day, and all vehicles must retain a particular carburetion setup, depending on the class. In the infancy of the class, racers did everything they could to squeeze more power out of their engines, but drivetrain modifications and weight reduction became the places to find quicker elapsed times.

Early Super Stockers were built from full-size passenger cars, such as the Chevrolet Impala or Ford Galaxie, but by 1964, Super Stock made a quick turn to the lighter platform of the newly created midsize sedans. Mopar had the market covered with its Dodge Coronet/Polara and Plymouth Belvedere/Sport Fury models, which were available with 426-ci Max Wedge engines (and later, Hemi engines), backed by

Super Stock classes created lots of buzz in the sport, and encouraged car manufacturers to build factory drag cars, such as the Ford Thunderbolt. This is the infamous *Strip Teaser* owned by Thomas Esso Oil Company and driven by Howard Neal. Small-time drag racers were soon touring the country on the Super Stock and match race circuits. (Photo Courtesy David Giles Collection)

Under the hood of this immaculately restored Dodge is a 426-ci Max Wedge engine, fit with dual Carter AFB carburetors atop a cross-ram intake manifold. This was a killer combination in the Super Stock class, and some racers preferred the Max Wedge over the outstanding new Hemi of the same displacement.

Chrysler Corporation played a huge role in the Super Stock game, producing cars that had amazing power and lightweight components. This 1964 Dodge 330 sports 12.5:1 compression and dual four-barrel carburetors right from the factory. It has been restored to original specifications. Drag cars were rarely as flawless as this restored Mopar, but this is a great example of a factory Super Stocker. These cars are still competitive in Super Stock ranks today.

very strong transmissions. Limited quantities of these performance-oriented cars were built as drag cars straight from the factory. Lightweight body panels and countless other weight-saving measures made these factory drag cars unbelievably quick, so a number of highly sought after race cars were running at tracks across the country. Mopar wasn't the only manufacturer in the game—Ford created a special Fairlane in 1964 and called it the Thunderbolt. Other manufacturers followed suit, causing the Super Stock class to grow tremendously.

Throughout the 1960s, car manufacturers began offering high-horsepower engine combinations, which made perfect Super Stock race cars. By the turn of the decade, the class had a wide variety of competitive combinations, while innovative racers and quick-shifting drivers made the racing action extremely close. Super Stock racing was particularly popular in the South, but other regions picked up on it and capitalized on the opportunity to draw a crowd. Rules were fairly simple, as the cars were divided based on their weight and claimed cubic inches.

You can safely assume that racers stretched the rules and found lots of loopholes in those early days, but that's what led to the evolution of the class and the sport. Racers didn't mind pushing the limits of their vehicles, so drag racing stayed fresh with new ideas, new cars, and fearless drivers. No matter the class, drag racing was a fierce competition in the 1960s, and innovation moved at a brisk pace.

Gassers and Altereds

Today, it's common for these two classes to be confused because of their similar qualities, but they were very different machines in the golden era of drag racing. The reason for the confusion is the fact that the term "gasser" has become a household description for any car with a nose-high stance. So, when someone sees a car that sits high, with radiused rear wheel openings, they assume it's a gasser, when it could very well be considered an altered. Regardless of the modern-day confusion, these two classes have produced some of the wildest drag cars in the history of the sport.

Classes had rules and regulations using the letter system (e.g., B/Gas, A/Altered, etc.), which was determined by the engine displacement and weight of the car. Even with these rules, the Gas and Altered classes looked like the outlaws of the sport from the average fan's perspective. From the driver's perspective, it was all highly competitive, even in the slower Gas and Altered classes, as the classes evolved at a quick rate.

At first, the Gas class was developed as an alternative to the Stock classes, which had specific rules against engine swaps or anything of that nature. In other words, "Stock" vehicles had to retain their original engines. Gas classes allowed you to stick a 392-ci Hemi engine in a Ford coupe, or any combination a racer could dream up. Obviously, this created a very unique class packed with wild setups. The most common Gas class car was a tossup between Willys coupes and the tri-five Chevy (1955, 1956, and 1957), but many racers really put

Chevrolet dominated the early days of Super Stock with its famed W engines. First, it came out with the 348 and then the 409-ci engine, but big news surrounded the debut of its Z-11 Impala in 1963. The Z-11 cars had a stroked 409- to 427-ci engine, all-aluminum front sheet metal, and other go-fast weight-saving options such as heater and radio delete (Photo Courtesy Ronnie Evans)

With the Super Stock class growing in popularity, many racers received great support from the manufacturers, in the form of factory drag cars. The "race on Sunday, sell on Monday" attitude was in full force during the 1960s when racers such as "Dandy" Dick Landy campaigned factory drag cars. (Photo Courtesy Bob Snyder)

Gassers came in all shapes and sizes—that's what set them apart from the other classes in drag racing. This is a typical gasser from the 1960s—straight-axle front suspension and radiused rear-wheel arches being the notable traits. Racers were split into classes by the total weight of their cars and the cubic-inch displacement of their engines. (Photo Courtesy Brent Fregin)

While most folks who jumped on the nostalgia bandwagon might consider this car a gasser because of its appearance, it wasn't allowed in the Gas class. Because of the drastic changes in the Corvair's drivetrain, it was forced to run in the Altered class. (Photo Courtesy Richard McFalls)

To be competitive in A/Gas, you needed a very quick car, as it was the top-dog class. To meet the regulations for the Gas classes, your car had to retain the original interior design with standard seating configuration, and it could have no more than 10-percent engine setback. (Photo Courtesy Larry Rose Collection)

their creative juices to work when it came time to build a gasser drag car. Throughout the years, the Gas classes evolved, and the Altered class was thrown into the mix, creating yet another division in the world of drag racing.

The main difference between the two classes was the amount of engine setback allowed, but other rules gave Altered class cars (simply called altereds) a bit more latitude, in terms of modifications. Gassers were allowed a 10-percent setback, meaning that the number-one sparkplug could be no more than 10 inches behind the front spindle centerline of a car with a 100-inch wheelbase. Altereds were allowed a 25-percent setback. The purpose of engine setback was to put more weight toward the rear of the vehicle.

Gassers were limited by seat location and a factory appearance of the interior. altereds could have a center-mounted seat with any type of interior modifications. Without question, Altered class cars had much more potential for speed, but the Gas classes placed no specific rules on engine combination, aside from the fact that it had to run on gasoline.

Funny Cars

The innovation of super stock cars led to factory experimental cars, which eventually led to the creation of "funny cars," originally named because of the comical looks of the altered-wheelbase design. Still holding onto the gasser mentality that a nose-high stance increased traction, the early funny cars had a very high center of gravity. This, in combination with the altered wheelbase and insane amounts of horsepower, made these volatile cars very fun to watch, and it didn't take long for the class to grow. Midsize cars, similar to those used in the Super Stock classes, were popular in the early days of the funny car ranks, and it was common to see very unique combinations on the track. Engine combinations that rivaled

Here's where the confusion begins: Many nostalgia drag racing enthusiasts think that a straight-axle front suspension and a nose-high stance means "gasser." While it was a very common trait of a gasser, many cars in the Altered class shared the same look. The main difference was engine setback—Gas allowed 10 percent and Altered allowed 25 percent.

As the Gas classes evolved, and other class structures formed, cars began to change dramatically. Gone were the days of straight-axle front suspension and a high center of gravity. By the mid 1970s, cars such as the *Chicken Coupe* raced in Gas classes but had different characteristics than cars of years prior.

As gassers, altereds, and super stockers evolved, a new class was born—A/FX (Altered Factory Experimental). This class was packed with mid-size sedans, most of which featured a wildly altered wheelbase, which created the nickname "funny car." These cars were crowd pleasers with wild passes and entertaining starting-line antics.

Cars like "Jungle" Jim's Camaro were fan favorites, but you didn't have to win lots of races to win over the crowd. Doing long burnouts and multiple dry hops gave spectators the ultimate drag racing experience—noise, fumes, and speed. This classic shot from York U.S. 30 shows a great, smoky burnout from Funny Car legend Jim Liberman. (Photo Courtesy Bob Snyder)

Only a few years after the creation of the class, A/FX cars had turned into what we now call funny cars, with custom tube frames, one-piece bodies, and Top Fuel–style engines. They were still fun to watch, and drew crowds to drag strips in every corner of the country on a weekly basis. (Photo Courtesy Bob Snyder)

Top Fuel powerplants gave these funny cars a mind of their own, and the drivers worked hard behind the wheel, skating on the edge of control.

These cars quickly evolved, moving away from the stock-style frames and transitioned to purpose-built tube frames. The tubular chassis design was much lighter, and while some folks kept the original skin of their respective cars, custom fiberglass bodies greatly reduced weight and improved aerodynamics. From there, it was only a matter of time before one-piece, flip-top bodies were considered the norm for funny cars. The concept of a pivoting body is pretty much the only thing that hasn't changed in the Funny Car world.

Although the competition aspect created lots of buzz, the showmanship of the drivers kept folks coming back to see the funny cars, and these driving techniques helped develop fan favorites and rivalries. Of course, there were always the popular Ford versus Chevy battles, but fans also liked particular drivers. A fan favorite didn't have to win all the time, so if a driver did the longest burnouts, made the wildest passes, and had the hottest back-up girl, he'd get lots of attention, which generally meant he would be scheduled for more match races and invited to big Funny Car meets. It was hard to deny the popularity of Funny Cars and the class withstood the test of time, as it continues to be a crowd pleaser to this day.

Decades ago, be it a thirty-two-car sanctioned event or a two-car match race, funny car drivers put on a show and had a good time doing it. Other classes had great showmanship, but Funny Car was definitely the top class in this regard. The days of 1,000-foot burnouts, dry hops, staging battles, and other starting-line activities might be gone, but the spirit of Funny Cars is still alive and well. Obviously, it was a win-win for drag strip owners, as the intense action attracted a steady flow of spectators, which caused the racing community to grow exponentially. And as those fans grew older, they wanted drag cars of their own, so the sport certainly blossomed as the years passed.

More Speed and More Fun

In the infancy of drag racing, there was no such thing as track prep, aside from sweeping debris off the surface. This made for a low-maintenance facility, for the most part. Obvi-

Years went by, but funny cars still retained their cool factor. By the 1970s and even into the 1980s, funny cars were the hot ticket to getting booked for match races and participating in Quick 16–style events. This Kellison-bodied funny car owned by Dennis George, has the 1970s look nailed—gold wheels, velocity stacks, and a groovy paint job.

In the professional ranks, aerodynamics became a big topic of discussion as the cars began to make more power. Eventually, wedge-shaped bodies with exaggerated bodylines became the norm, and this Mustang II funny car at Marion County International Raceway in LaRue, Ohio is a great example of the trend. These days, funny cars have lost all their character and are barely recognizable when compared to the street cars they are supposed to represent.

ously, as the cars went faster, measures were taken to keep them glued to the racing surface. Today's traction compounds weren't available in the early days, so racers found ways to stay in control of the horsepower, rather than relying on the track to do the work for them. This lack of traction forced the introduction of purpose-built drag racing tires in the late 1950s, along with an endless list of components that are still in use on many of today's drag cars.

Even after the development of drag racing tires, the high-powered cars, especially in the fuel classes, spun the tires for the majority of the quarter mile. Smoke-screen passes were standard practice, and a regular burnout before a run was essentially unheard of until the 1960s. Without question, these tire-smoking passes made for exciting action, but it also made for a very high level of danger, as the cars were nearly out of control from start to finish. Crashes were fairly common, which is yet another bittersweet aspect of the golden years of drag racing—the unpredictability was great for spectators, but it came with a hefty price tag for the gearhead behind the wheel. When racers started figuring out how to keep their machines hooked up, speeds went up and elapsed times went down in a hurry.

Tires grew larger over the years, as tire engineers found new ways to soften the tread for increased traction. By this time, Firestone was a huge player in the drag tire game, alongside M&H Racemaster, pioneer of the drag racing tire. Like many forms of competition, necessity led to innovation, which allowed the sport and the industry to grow at a feverish pace. Unfortunately, today's big-money drag racing has reached a bit of a flat spot on the innovation graph, so to speak, although the cars continue to evolve in terms of safety.

Another factor that added to the fun of drag racing in the 1960s and 1970s was the diversity and entertainment value. Drag racing wasn't nearly as polished as it is these days, and that was a good thing. Drivers didn't know how to be a spokesman for their sponsors, aside from putting on the best show possible. TV interviews were the last thing on their mind. Back then, if your track didn't have the right con-

nections for a big points race or something of that nature, you picked up the phone and set up a match race. It was the perfect scenario for small, outlaw tracks because they could draw a great crowd of spectators without all of the regulations required in sanctioned racing.

It was also a great experience for spectators, as it allowed them to pick a favorite, usually based on the make of the car. Ford versus Chevy has long been the most prominent battle of the brands, but there were lots of big players in those days. The big three (Ford, Chevy, and Mopar) were heavy hitters, but you couldn't count out the other brands of the era when it came to making power.

The cars, in general, weren't all that fast compared to the rocket ships of the modern era, but they didn't leave anything on the table. No matter the class, racers used every ounce of power they had, and put it all on the line with every single pass.

It was quite common for regular street cars to see action on the drag strip, but it took a skilled driver to be competitive in a class of race-prepped vehicles. This 1964 Corvette has a 327-ci engine, rated from the factory at 365 hp, backed by a Muncie M21 four-speed manual transmission and a 4.11:1 rear gear ratio.

Traction was hard to find in the old days. Racers often resorted to their own form of traction compound, commonly referred to as "gold dust." The racer's crew sprinkled the rosin on the track, making sure the rear tires passed through it during the burnout. Here, at Drag City in Ringgold, Georgia, some dust is applied. (Photo Courtesy Wayne Holland)

The amazing growth of drag racing made it a very popular hobby, even with the inherent danger that always lurks around these unbelievably fast racing machines. During the 1950s, drag racing caught on quickly, causing a ripple effect in the car guy community. Casual fans watched the action and eventually wanted to try their hand at it, which made the hobby grow exponentially. Gearheads became enthralled with the idea of going quicker and faster every time they hit the track, and it was truly a time of excitement as records fell on a regular basis. The various sanctioning bodies offered great racing across the country, but the wildly popular sport eventually felt the effects of its rapid growth.

Safety

Home-built hot rods and dragsters evolved greatly during the late 1940s and early 1950s, but this ingenuity didn't include a great deal of safety equipment. During the first full decade of drag racing, most serious injuries and fatalities were caused by rollover accidents, which either ejected or entrapped the driver. There are lots of stories of throttles sticking, causing cars to careen out of control, and fire was also a big enemy of the early drag racers.

Pushing an engine to the limit revealed the weak points of the components, while the driveline parts faced a tough battle

This photo was taken in 1957 at San Fernando Valley Drag Strip and perfectly illustrates the creative side of dragster building. With a longer wheelbase than most cars of the era, and a blown Olds sporting a primitive two-port fuel injection setup, this car was probably a hot topic in the pits. (Photo Courtesy Larry Rose Collection)

Unfortunately, racer creativity didn't often go hand in hand with safety, which resulted in numerous injuries and fatalities in the early days of drag racing. Poor track conditions, combined with lots of horsepower made for unpredictable races—exactly what the crowd wanted to see. This Ford sedan at Brainerd Optimist Drag Strip in Tennessee didn't fare too well, but its driver walked away! (Photo Courtesy Larry Rose Collection)

Yet another example of the no-rules attitude is brought to life with this home-built Crosley-powered dragster, making a pass at Oswego Dragway in the late 1950s. Obviously, the car didn't make much power, but the driver still took a big risk by squeezing himself into the tiny cockpit. (Photo Courtesy Norbert Locke)

as well. Clutch explosions were fairly common in the early days, as stock clutch sets couldn't quite withstand the intense engine RPM, additional horsepower, and unruly driving style. Without the assistance of a scatter shield, these early clutch explosions wreaked havoc on a drag racing car, with shrapnel going in every direction, often shearing fuel lines. Massive fires and violent crashes took the lives of many early drag racers, but it was all a large part of learning the importance of safety in this swiftly growing sport.

The first in a long line of safety measures taken was the infamous "fuel ban" policed by the NHRA for all of its sanctioned tracks. Racers experimented with a number of volatile fuels, but the most prominent was (and still is) nitromethane. The difference between this fuel and gasoline is the way it burns inside the engine. Racers quickly figured out that an engine could consume a lot more nitromethane than gasoline

during a single combustion cycle. For instance, the perfect air/fuel ratio for a gasoline engine is 14.6 parts air and 1 part fuel, while a nitro-burning engine is much closer to a 1:1 ratio. This means a violent explosion in the combustion chambers that helps make incredible horsepower. Due to a number of fires and accidents, Wally Parks and the NHRA placed a ban on nitromethane in 1957, which was like throwing out an anchor to slow down the racing world.

During the NHRA fuel ban, the AHRA allowed nitro cars to compete, giving all those folks a place to race. While the big guns moved to the AHRA circuit, those dedicated to the NHRA were forced to up the ante with various engine combinations and unique experiments. Multiple engines were popular for the dragster crowd, but superchargers quickly stole the show by multiplying the engine's horsepower without the aid of exotic fuels. The addition of nitro to a supercharged engine

While some dragsters were crude by nature, others such as the *Nesbitt's Orange Special*, featured masterful workmanship. Built by Bob Armstrong and driven by Maurice Richer, this dragster was a top-notch piece in its day. A Hilborn-injected Chrysler Hemi powered the dragster, motivating it to mid-9-second passes at more than 155 mph. (Photo Courtesy Larry Rose Collection)

During the NHRA's ban on nitromethane fuel, racers had to find new ways of making horsepower. Superchargers came onto the scene and made huge gains, but many racers, including Norbert Locke, went with the "two is better than one" mindset and coupled two engines together. His dragster (here at Oswego) featured twin blown flatheads! (Photo Courtesy Norbert Locke)

Some of the wild race cars were built in the name of true competition, while others, such as this four engine, four-wheel-drive dragster, were built as exhibition vehicles. "TV Tommy" Ivo built this Buick-powered dragster and thrilled crowds across the country by smoking all four tires the entire length of the track. Poor vision and unbelievable torque steer made this a very dangerous machine. (Photo Courtesy Norbert Locke)

unleashed a new level of power and speed. The NHRA lifted the fuel ban before the 1964 season began.

With the increasing speeds, it was up to drag strip owners and operators to update their facilities to accommodate the action. There are different stories about the first 200-mph pass in a fuel dragster, but by the mid 1960s, it seemed to be an ordinary task for the top drivers of the sport. Big-time drag strips quickly adapted to the insane speeds and unpredictable nature of drag cars by installing guardrails, limiting spectator access, and prioritizing driver safety. While the outlaw atmosphere of drag racing was reduced by the ever-evolving rulebook and safety regulations, it ultimately saved a lot of lives

The freedom to walk around in the pits and close to the race track made outlaw tracks a big hit, as here at Harriman Drag Strip. (Photo Courtesy Ray Bunn)

Paradise Drag Strip, an outlaw track in Calhoun, Georgia, always had huge events, but was never sanctioned by any of the major associations. Here *Poison Dart* and *Dr. Feelgood* go head to head.

Generally, large purses brought out lots of racers, which, in turn, brought out lots of spectators. Events such as the AHRA Summer Nationals, held at New York National Speedway, always attracted huge crowds because the general public knew that all the big dogs would be in town. (Photo Courtesy Bob Snyder)

With experimental engine and transmission combinations, parts failures were quite common during the first few decades of drag racing. This 1957 Chevy at Oswego Dragway experienced a major clutch explosion, which left it with a broken windshield and a mangled cowl and dash. These accidents were terribly dangerous for the drivers, but also put the spectators and track crew at risk. (Photo Courtesy Brent Fregin)

In the mid 1960s, competitive class-based drag racing was still affordable for the average working man. Even with low budget racers, many guys teamed up with friends or family to form a small racing team. By splitting the budget, it made racing much more affordable, and proved to be one of the attractive aspects of the hobby. This race took place at Drag City in Georgia. (Photo Courtesy Richard McFalls)

This sight became all too normal for drag strips across America. The gates are closed, weeds are growing, and there hasn't been any sign of activity in years—this is how many abandoned drag strips appear today, unfortunately. The pavement in the background hasn't been used since the 1980s, and there is no chance of the track reopening.

n the professional circuit. However, the professional circuits (NHRA and AHRA) only accounted for a fraction of the rag racing activities in the United States, meaning that many rag strips fell behind the times, in terms of safety equipment.

Unsanctioned drag strips are often referred to as "out-law tracks" because of their no-rules attitude, and these tracks ctually made an impact on the sport. The outlaw tracks pro-ided a place to race for those who couldn't make the trek to a rofessionally sanctioned drag strip, and the no-holds-barred acing mindset made for some interesting innovations. The outheast drag racing scene is famous almost entirely because f its outlaw roots, which eventually produced a host of drag acing legends.

Although outlaw tracks catered to the grassroots guys, rack managers and promoters were not afraid to put up a big urse to draw a bunch of racers and spectators. Super Stock nd Funny Car races were huge events for hometown tracks, you didn't have to live near a high-dollar facility to see the g names of the sport. These tracks also set up incredible atch races, which kept the popular drag racers quite busy the 1960s.

All across the country, track promoters created flyers, ade radio commercials, and generated all sorts of hype to ring folks in the gate—and it worked. Huge crowds gathered

for these events, which eventually caused safety concerns. The close proximity of spectators at the outlaw tracks combined with the unpredictability of the wild drivers turned out to be the biggest drawback of all. Both the drivers' and the specta-tors' lives were in danger and it was only a matter of time before injuries and deaths put a damper on the sport.

Southern tracks suffered the most from the inherent dan-gers of drag racing, as the tracks and race cars generally had a bit more homegrown flavor than some of the bigger tracks. Accidents became more common as the cars outgrew the tracks, and it caused many Southern venues to close their gates by the late 1960s.

The Economy

Fast forward another ten years, and the number of outlaw tracks had dwindled even further. A bad economic outlook on the shoulders of the oil crisis caused devastation to many drag racers and spectators. The mid and late 1970s were a particu-larly bad time for drag racing, as the harsh economy caused a general lack of interest in high-performance cars. In 1975, the most powerful American car on the market barely made 200 hp, so these lifeless cars became the norm, as did a number of atrocious "economy" cars.

As time went on, drag racing became more expensive for the "average Joe" wanting to race a souped-up production car, which meant entries quickly dropped off and spectator numbers soon followed. With the muscle car era in the rearview mirror, the only racers who stayed with the hobby were the ones who could afford to play. The days of bolting a pair of slicks to a stock Chevelle were over because the sport of drag racing had evolved to the point of out-pricing its participants. The professional ranks continued to go quicker and faster, thanks to the aid of sponsors and high-dollar racing teams, but grassroots racing all but ended when the muscle car era came to a close.

Big events at big tracks retained the interest of spectators for several more years, but eventually even the big events lost their appeal to the general public, as the number of car enthusiasts continued to shrink with each passing day. When the car hobby dried up, so did sponsorship dollars. By the late 1970s and early 1980s, drag strips had a tough time staying in business. Even tracks with high-dollar contracts with the big sanctioning bodies could barely afford to stay open. A particularly difficult time for drag racing came in 1978, as a large number of tracks closed due to poor attendance and participation.

Without question, the car hobby didn't completely die during those tough times, but many tracks simply couldn't sit back and wait for the industry to resurrect itself. Drag strips quickly became hot items in the real estate business, providing plenty of room for housing communities, industrial buildings,

or retail buildings. Even if a track changed hands with the hope of resuming the racing action, many had been grandfathered in to noise and other local ordinances, which leads us to the next reason for widespread track closures in the United States.

Population and Politics

Parts of the United States suffered from various effect of growing populations and/or the influence of local politics. The West and some parts of the Northeast had an exploding population, which caused major problems for local track that were simply overtaken by suburban growth. Other were claimed by the industrial growth that accompanied the increased population. It was a no-win situation for drag strip across the country, as functioning tracks were sold to developers who didn't waste any time disposing of the track and bulldozing local racers' hopes in the process.

Many West Coast drag strips were taking up valuable real estate in the 1970s, so land developers made land owners an offer they couldn't refuse. If the actual title holders had been drag racers at heart, the outcome may have been different, but many tracks were built on leased property, so dollar amounts could easily sway the owner's opinion of drag racing.

Industrial development caused several tracks to close, but it came down to individuals for many other closures. By that I mean individuals who complained to their local law officials and forced new rules to hurt the track's business in an effort

In the 1970s, the hot rod and drag racing industry fell on hard times due to an ailing economy. With people struggling for money, it left no budget for racing, which killed a number of tracks. The year of the most track closures seems to be 1978, but the late 1970s and early 1980s also proved to be a tough time for racers. This run was at Drag City. (Photo Courtesy Bob Snyder)

Noise complaints are normal for drag strips, which has been true since the early days. The cars are naturally loud, because they have lots of compression, big camshafts, and very large headers. With no mufflers, any drag car is quite loud, but when you add nitromethane to the mix, the noise is incredible. I still don't understand why everyone doesn't love it.

...o get it shut down for good. Politics killed a lot of drag strips, ...nd it's one of the big reasons most tracks close today.

The type of politics associated with race tracks are gener-...lly town governments and organizations that band together ...o stop a particular function—like drag racing and the noise ...hat goes along with it. When the initial buzz of drag racing ...vent away, the complaints started rolling in on a regular basis. ...t was an unfortunate "black eye" for the sport, which thrives ...n all things loud, fast, and dangerous. Quiet, slow, and safe ...doesn't quite have the same appeal. So, as the years went on, ...rack owners could no longer ignore the requests made by ...ocal officials, which meant strict curfews and a limited num-

...ber of events per year. These actions did just as much damage to the drag racing community as the fatal crashes and the bad economy. A significant number of small circle tracks suffered this same fate.

Many of the complainers were folks who moved into the area long after the track was constructed, leaving them without a logical argument, at least in the eyes of most racers. If you move near a drag strip or circle track, you could expect to hear a great deal of noise on the weekends—seems simple, right? As we all know, logic has no place in politics, so many drag strip neighbors got their way by contacting the right people to get the job done. County commissioners, mayors, and other city officials played a big part in closing many race facilities, which wasn't just limited to drag strips. Other race tracks have also felt the pain of noise complaints, but drag racing definitely wins the decibel contest, especially in areas where the sound could carry for many miles. The end result of all this drama between tracks and local governments was a drastic reduction in the number of functioning race tracks in the United States.

Politics caused many drag strips to shut down, and it's been a problem for many years. In fact, it's one of the leading causes of drag strip closures in the modern era, and it's mainly related to noise complaints from nearby neighbors, as here at Green Valley Raceway Drag Strip in Smithfield, Texas. (Photo Courtesy Steve Scott)

Moving On

Some gearheads simply hung up their helmets and never raced again when their home track was shut down, while others decided to travel more often to find places to race. The lack of hometown drag strips forced the diehard guys to step up into the professional ranks, which played a large role in creating the high-class world of drag racing we're left with today. It's great to see drag racing as a legitimate motorsport, but when it's more of a business plan than a pastime, it takes having fun out of the equation.

These days, sponsor dollars take precedent over the showmanship that once powered the sport, at least in the professional ranks. Nostalgia drag racing has brought back some of those great qualities from the 1960s and 1970s, but it will never be the same, no matter how hard we try. The professional ranks (i.e., Top Fuel, Funny Car, Pro Stock) are dead in the water in terms of entertainment value, because every car is nearly identical to the next, every driver is overly concerned with sponsor obligations, and every pass down the strip costs more than most folks make in a month. Imagine scattering a $50,000 engine and going into the trailer and grabbing another one to make the next round. With that mindset, there's no

such thing as grassroots or entry level, so it's easy to see why the sport has been in a relatively downward spiral in the eye of longtime drag racers and hardcore gearheads.

So, what happened to racers who couldn't afford to keep up with the big dogs? Some of them raced on different circuits, such as the International Hot Rod Association (IHRA) while others sold off all of their go-fast equipment and moved on to a different hobby. There are a select few who held on to their cars and speed parts, hoping for a breath of fresh air to revive the spirit of the good ol' days.

That resuscitating breath came in the form of nostalgia drag racing, which started in the late 1980s. It inspired many retired car guys and racers to pull their defunct drag cars out of the barn and put them back on the track. It also gave hope to thousands of neglected cars.

While some car guys blew the dust off their old hot rod and supported the nostalgia drag racing scene, others were past the point of return. Despite the lack of interest, it's still a big deal to find the whereabouts of an old race car, so the barn find craze has certainly rejuvenated a number of retired drag racers. There are still hundreds, if not thousands, of abandoned drag cars across the country that have yet to be unearthed, some of which may be right under our noses.

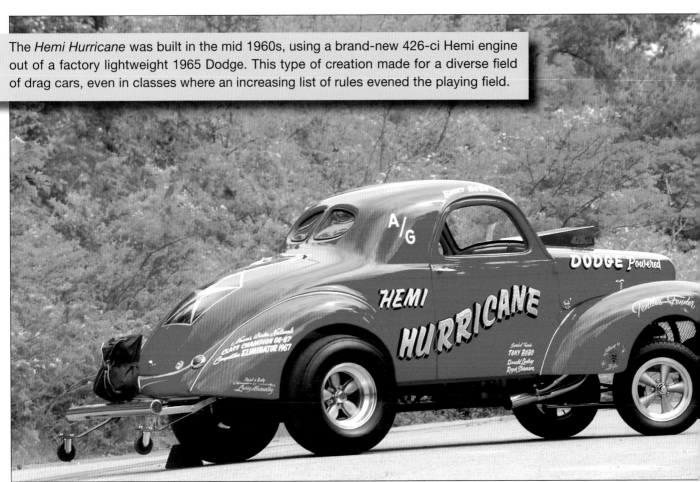

The *Hemi Hurricane* was built in the mid 1960s, using a brand-new 426-ci Hemi engine out of a factory lightweight 1965 Dodge. This type of creation made for a diverse field of drag cars, even in classes where an increasing list of rules evened the playing field.

When drag strips went through tough times in the early 1970s, many racers were forced to hang up their helmets and move on to a different hobby. Bunky Bobo and Frank Groves built this 1940 Willys in the mid 1960s, and then Bobo's son Tony restored the Hemi-powered coupe forty years later to perfectly match its former glory.

During the 1960s, the Deuce coupe went through a few changes, such as the higher ride height, but the one to the left is documented to be the original car seen in the vintage photo above. The car is pictured here at a swap meet, with an asking price of $32,000. A fully documented vintage drag car like this with local history demands big money these days.

You won't find a more classic drag racing photo than this one at Brainerd Optimist Drag Strip. It features a blown 1940 Ford Deluxe coupe squaring off against a 1932 Ford coupe with the flagman in mid-jump. After the drag racing scene dried up a bit, the 1932 Ford was sold off, where it went into hibernation for more than forty years. (Photo Courtesy Larry Rose Collection)

The Alternative

In the early 1970s, the closing of countless drag strips resulted in an effort to find alternative places to race, as a great number of competitors had their home tracks taken away. It was normal to see a drag strip on the pit road of a NASCAR speedway, but these pit-road drag strips rarely offered a full quarter mile of racing surface. Most of the time, pit-road strips were eighth mile in length, while a select few actually had the real estate to go the full quarter.

Even then, at tracks such as Ontario Motor Speedway in California, the burnout box wasn't in line with the racing surface, requiring burnouts in what were staging lanes at a conventional drag strip. Although it had an odd burnout area, Ontario was a big-time facility, mainly because it catered to so many racing organizations. It hosted NASCAR events, NHRA events, as well as Formula One and other open-wheel events. It had a 2½-mile oval track, a quarter-mile drag strip, and an infield road course that was more than 4 miles in length.

Decades of abuse from Mother Nature took its toll on the *Satisfaction* 1955 Chevy, but local car guy Scott Abbott dug it out of the weeds anyway. Although the car was rusty from top to bottom, Abbott stuffed a big-block V-8 between the fenders, and got it running again. The car was a huge hit at nostalgia drag events.

Dennis Hefner stands with his B/Gas-prepared 1955 Chevy 210 at Harriman Drag Strip. A straight front axle, radiused rear-wheel openings, and blue lexan windows were popular Gasser items, and this 1955 had them all. Hefner campaigned the car for several years before he retired from drag racing. (Photo Courtesy David Giles Collection)

Although various drag racing events were held on the pit lane of many speedways, this trend didn't last. Some tracks still hold "street drags" on pit road, but it's generally a test-and-tune atmosphere, geared toward street cars.

Another way to take advantage of multiple forms of racing in a single facility is to incorporate a drag strip in a road course. A good example of this is Infineon Raceway in Sonoma, California, which features an NHRA-sanctioned, quarter-mile drag strip within the confines of its 900-acre racing course. The big road course is home to one of NASCAR's only road courses used in the Sprint Cup series. There are still several motorsports parks that feature a drag strip, as well as another racing course, but Infineon is unique because the drag strip is actually inside the borders of the road course track, rather being than a separate entity.

Although many racers and entrepreneurs have banded together to build drag strips, it's much more difficult. Stories of tracks being closed greatly outnumber stories of brand-new drag racing facilities. One of the biggest news stories to hit the drag racing world in the past decade was the unveiling of Z-Max Dragway, located in Charlotte, North Carolina. This is Charlotte's first drag strip since Shuffletown Drag Strip closed in the early 1990s, so the NASCAR-crazed city welcomed it with open arms. The new four-lane drag strip has been extremely popular.

There were many old-time drag racers who quit racing, but never sold any of their hard-earned equipment. One such case is Milburn Varner.

Like many young men, Varner began drag racing in the late 1950s. He started with a Pontiac, but quickly moved his focus to Mopar as he became more serious about going fast. Varner found a racing partner, who turned out to be his brother-in-law, David Rehring, and the two ate, drank, and slept drag racing for more than a decade. They started with a Max Wedge–powered 1963 Plymouth Belvedere.

Racing in the Super Stock ranks during the 1960s, they had plenty of choices when it came to drag strips, so they traveled to local tracks and battled it out with like-minded racers. They moved on to other Mopar-sourced drag machines over the next few years, but the focus here is their 1970 Plymouth 'Cuda. Instead of moving on, Varner decided to simply park this race car, as well as an abundance of Mopar speed parts.

Purchased new from Austin Motors in Chattanooga, the 1970 'Cuda entered Varner's life as a Plum Crazy–colored 440 Six-Pack car. He says that it was the infamous 1970 Chevelle convertible Super Stocker driven by Ray Allen that motivated him to up the ante among the local Super Stock ranks. That blue Chevelle broke records, won countless races, and set the Super Stock world on its ear. Varner's only answer was a four-letter word that Mopar owners are very familiar with—Hemi.

This is where the story gets interesting, as Varner's donor car of choice was a 1967 Plymouth GTX convertible; yes, a Hemi convertible. One of seventeen built, the rarity of the GTX didn't mean much to Varner at the time, so the engine was plucked and transplanted into the 'Cuda. With only a handful of passes and exactly 149 street miles, the original 440 Six-Pack engine now sits on a stand in Varner's basement.

The beauty of all this is that he still has the 'Cuda, as well as the GTX convertible. He also has the old 1963 Max Wedge car, as well as another 1966 Belvedere factory Hemi car, so to say he's a diehard Mopar guy would be a gross understatement. His love for racing is still as strong as ever, but Varner and his racing partner stopped racing in 1973, after twelve straight years of the drag racing life.

A typical drag car from the early 1970s, this Plymouth 'Cuda belonged to Milburn Varner and David Rehring, who raced in the Super Stock ranks. Though it was originally a 440 Six-Pack car, the eager gearheads swapped in a Hemi engine shortly after buying the car. Varner claims they quit drag racing due to being priced out of competition. (Photo Courtesy David Giles Collection)

The Drag Addicts 'Cuda was parked in 1973, and it still sits in Varner's garage, unaltered from its racing days. The 426-ci Hemi is intact, as is the original 440 Six-Pack engine, which only has a few hundred miles on it. Varner still loves drag racing but admits it was way more fun in the 1960s and early 1970s.

During the 1970s, many oval tracks held drag races on their pit road. One was Charlotte Motor Speedway. The pit road was home of the 1974 IHRA Southern Nationals, which was reported to be the first eighth-mile national event. Unfortunately, the drag racing was short-lived, due in part to Dave Anderson's fatal crash aboard the *Pollution Packer* rocket-powered dragster. (Photo Courtesy Bob Snyder)

Ontario Motor Speedway in California was another great example of a track that really made pit road racing work. Unfortunately, the entire facility shut down in 1980, even though it was sanctioned by NASCAR, NHRA, USAC, and FIA, the four most prominent sanctioning bodies in the racing world. (Photo Courtesy Bob Snyder)

It's not often that new drag strips are built, but the Z-Max Dragway in Concord, North Carolina, is a top-of-the-line facility in every aspect. With four lanes of racing action, it made big news in the drag racing world by running four-wide Top Fuel and Funny Cars at its first NHRA event.

Believe it or not, there was once a time when a guy on the East Coast didn't have direct access to the best speed parts of the era. There was no Internet, no lightning-fast shipping capabilities, and no parts warehouses with millions of components on the shelf, ready to ship. Getting parts from California carried huge bragging rights, and it generally meant you would ultimately be faster than the guy without the fancy speed equipment.

These days, we're accustomed to worldwide access to all of the high-end parts our wallet can handle, but this wasn't the case in the early days of drag racing. That's why most folks say that the West Coast was light-years ahead of the racers back East, even though the extreme ingenuity of the Northeastern and Southern racers made up for the lack of technology and parts availability. Without question, California was the place to be during the golden era of drag racing, as it was packed with diehard racers and lots of big-name engine builders, parts manufacturers, and well-equipped drag strips.

It all started with the Santa Ana Drags in 1950, which was nothing more than an unused portion of the Orange County Airport with some cobbled-together timing equipment. The track was the first of its kind, and it created a demand for more facilities across the state of California, while setting standards that are still in effect today. As racers heard about the first official drag strip, they banded together to create more places to race, and by the beginning of the next decade there was a multitude of drag strips.

Southern California was definitely the hotspot, with drag strips popping up all over. Fontana, Carlsbad, and Pomona are only a few of the popular tracks in SoCal, with the most memorable being Lions Associated Drag Strip in Long Beach. Other extremely popular tracks built during the 1960s were Irwindale Raceway in the San Gabriel Valley and Orange County International Raceway in Irvine, neither of which survived the test of time.

So, why did the boom in drag racing popularity result in such an unfortunate end? For the West Coast, and more

The drag racing scene exploded on the West Coast during the 1950s and quickly spread. By the late 1950s, dragsters were quite common and put on an incredible show for the spectators, while also giving the driver a great thrill. Those tiny slicks didn't stand a chance of hooking up, but that's the way they liked it. (Photo Courtesy Larry Rose Collection)

Southern California was the ultimate drag racing hotspot, with several big-time tracks in the vicinity. Moving into the late 1960s, drag racing had evolved greatly thanks to a number of innovative gearheads. Mickey Thompson was one of the best, and this is one of his many drag cars doing its thing at Lions. (Photo Courtesy Don Gillespie Collection)

Dragsters and funny cars were very popular on the West Coast, with track promoters regularly holding huge events. This was a big draw for spectators, as the top-dog cars always had great fan appeal. Some tracks had as many as sixty-four funny cars on hand for a single event! (Photo Courtesy Don Gillespie Collection)

specifically Southern California, it was all about population growth and city expansion. With neighborhoods, schools, hospitals, and shopping centers being built at a feverish pace, the cities could no longer afford to allow acres of land to "go to waste." During the 1970s, hard economic times and the rising costs of racing competitively drove many drag strips out of business, but the increasing safety regulations and city ordinances also caused a great number of drag strip closures.

Southern California had more than twenty drag strips, but that number is drastically lower these days. The only real survivor is Pomona, which is now called Auto Club Raceway, located in the massive Los Angeles County Fairplex. It's a major NHRA-sanctioned drag strip that hosts the Winternationals (the first event of the NHRA Full Throttle Drag Racing season) as well as the Auto Club Finals (the final event of the season).

Other parts of the Western region took advantage of the momentum carried by the great number of racers in the SoCal area. Surrounding states held regular drag races at a variety of legitimate drag strips, with popularity growing in the 1960s, just as it did in California. Drag strips, such as Bee Line Dragway in Scottsdale, Arizona, had great success, but due to a number of reasons could not survive. With ultra-flat land and wide-open spaces, building a drag strip in Arizona proved to be rather easy, but that didn't mean the folks in the mountainous land of Colorado hesitated to build drag strips as well. The urge to provide a place to race was evident across the country, but it definitely got its start west of the Rocky Mountains.

North and east of California, drag strips appeared frequently, giving car guys a place to race without breaking the law. Washington, Oregon, and Nevada had their share of strips in the heyday of drag racing, but fell to the same troubles as the legendary tracks featured in this chapter. It's safe to say that drag racing out West had its advantages in the early days of the sport, but racers from the other side of the country made quick work of leveling the playing field.

Huge races with incredible car counts and thousands of spectators gave these Western tracks a very strong reputation, but it wasn't enough to keep them alive during a tough time for the sport in general. With fewer places to race, the fellows who couldn't afford to travel eventually gave up on the hobby, which created a vicious cycle of retiring racers and decaying tracks. The result is hundreds of abandoned and repurposed drag strips across the country, hiding in the shadows of today's big-money professional drag racing series. In the case of most California drag strips, the property didn't sit abandoned for long. Real estate is extremely valuable in California, so it didn't make sense for all those acres to lay idle.

While it's sad to see these hallowed grounds in such poor shape, it's important to remember the good times, when drag racing was simple, fun, and exciting for everyone involved. Even if you aren't old enough to have experienced the good times at these legendary racing facilities, it's easy to see how drag racing became a major motorsport in such a short period of time. The pictures could tell a story all by themselves, but the tales of great innovation, wild action, and unbelievable sportsmanship explain the fascination with West Coast drag racing, as it thrived in the 1950s, 1960s, and 1970s.

Unfortunately, the large number of drag strips on the West Coast meant that as interest in drag racing declined, a significant number of tracks closed. Many tracks met their demise due to the vast urbanization of California, as well as skyrocketing property values. Seen here is all that remains of Fremont Drag Strip (Baylands Raceway), which closed in 1988. (Photo Courtesy David Giles)

LIONS ASSOCIATED DRAG STRIP

A vintage aerial view of Lions shows its unique seating arrangement, which provided a great view for thousands of spectators at every event. In some areas, the seating was extremely close to the action, making it a thrilling experience for the spectators, while also adding an always-exciting element of danger. (Photo Courtesy Don Gillespie Collection)

Wilmington, California
1955-1972

Current Status: ➤ SHIPPING YARD

Whether you referred to it as the Beach, LADS, or simply Lions, no one can deny that Lions Associated Drag Strip was *the* destination for drag racers in the heyday of the hobby. It was a premier track and it certainly left a lasting impression on thousands of performance-minded fellows during its time in operation, so it ranks highly in the world of nostalgia. Many memories, good and bad, were made at Lions, and it certainly went out with a bang, so let's dig into what made this track so special.

The idea of building a drag strip spawned from a Long Beach judge, Fred Miller, who believed that a legitimate drag strip would reduce the urge to race on the street. A meeting with well-known gearhead Mickey Thompson put the process into motion. For a short time, the track was known as Harbor Area Drag Strip, but it was most commonly known as Lions

Associated Drag Strip because the Los Angeles area Lions clubs were the only associations to raise funds for the building of the track. The $45,000 they raised to build the track didn't quite cut it, so the crew of volunteers took a gamble and pressed on. After working out some of the preliminary

It's hard to get any cooler than this old Lions Drag Strip logo with its roaring lion and dragster illustration. Lions will go down in history as one of the greatest drag strips of all time, and with good reason, as it was the go-to drag strip for racers from 1955 to its final race held in 1972. (Photo Courtesy Don Gillespie Collection)

Plentiful parking and staging areas made Lions a great place for big races, which in tur[n] made it an all-time favorite for racing fans. This photo from 1966 shows the legenda[ry] track's general landscape, including the catwalk, which gave spectators a great view of th[e] action that only a few other tracks could provide. (Photo Courtesy Don Gillespie Collection[)]

Mickey Thompson was Lions Associated Drag Strip's first paid employee, serving as the track manager for several years. His passion for drag racing made him the perfect fit as manager. He also built numerous drag cars during his time at the helm. Thompson later handed off the management duties to legendary track promoter C. J. "Pappy" Hart. (Photo Courtesy Don Gillespie Collection)

details, the deal was struck, and the Los Angeles Harbor Commission leased an unused railyard to the Lions Club on a thirty-day revocable basis. Mickey Thompson was the only paid employee, working as the track manager until the mid 1960s. All proceeds from the track went to charities, as designated by local Lions Club chapters.

On October 9, 1955, Lions Associated Drag Strip held its first event. The track crew expected a large crowd, but when the tally of spectators soared north of 10,000, it certainly overwhelmed the workers. The first event proved its worth, but it took a few years to get the bugs worked out. By 1957, lights had been installed at the track, allowing night racing, which was a huge hit. Lions drew large crowds for its big races, but it also had a great following with its street car and grudge racing events, so it was a well-rounded facility with a certain flair that was never duplicated.

Part of the unforgettable atmosphere was the fact that its location near the Pacific Ocean offered something that can only be described as "rare air." The track was at sea level, so it already had an advantage, but the dense air from the nearby ocean gave it a reputation as one of the quickest and fastest tracks in the country. It was truly a destination for racers and spectators from across the country.

The famous 30-foot-long Lions Drag Strip sign is an iconic symbol. It served as a wonderful background for thousands of action photos such as this one, featuring the legendary Greer/Black/Prudhomme dragster in the near lane, with Chris Karamesines' *Chizler* pulling ahead in the far lane. (Photo Courtesy Don Gillespie Collection)

From the other side of the track, you can see the steepness of the spectator seating. "Big John" Mazmanian rips off the line in his well-known supercharged gas Willys coupe, which perfectly embodies the gasser styling we all know and love. (Photo Courtesy Don Gillespie Collection)

In 1965, a new class hit the AHRA circuit and i quickly spread to all tracks and sanctioning bod ies. Cars in the new Altered Factory Experimenta (A/FX) class featured an altered wheelbase and virtually unlimited engine combinations. Here, Dic Harrell (in the near lane) and Dale Armstrong leave the line. (Photo Courtesy Don Gillespie Collection

Through the years, drag racing grew by leaps and bounds with innovative drag cars being debuted at nearly every major event. In the end, the traditional single-engine drag ster setup (such as this Ries/Chambers/Murphy example topped all of the experimental builds until Don Garlits per fected the rear-engine design after his accident at Lions i 1970. (Photo Courtesy Don Gillespie Collection)

Under the management of Mickey Thompson, Lions Drag Strip set the standard for all strips, with its timing system and what is now affectionately known as the Christmas tree. Though not as sophisticated as today's tree, the starting system at Lions did away with the flagman starter, which made great strides to legitimize the sport. When it was time to resign from track management and focus on his other business ventures, Mickey Thompson passed the torch to C. J. "Pappy" Hart, who ran the facility and helped develop a number of classes, including Jr. Fuel.

Pappy was instrumental in the drag racing world, so it was only fitting for him to manage the country's premier track during the height of its popularity. He worked hard to keep the track in top form, experimenting with various coatings to enhance traction. Pappy went as far as snagging a chunk of pavement from the defunct San Gabriel Drag Strip to analyze for research.

Steve Evans took over management of Lions in 1972, and worked with the NHRA to hold its Grand Premiere event a the legendary track. Records fell during the NHRA event, and the non-stop action kept spectators buzzing, so Steve was o the right track for a successful term as track manager.

Late in 1972, the Harbor Commission revoked the thirty day lease agreement with no warning. Neither the Lions Clul nor any of the track's supporters could stop the quick-movin Harbor Commission, which stated the reason was increasin noise complaints. The truth of the matter was that the prop erty was a valuable asset to the Commission, and it had a opportunity to make a large profit by utilizing the property t its full potential. Months later, the track was transformed int a warehouse and shipping yard, but not before one of the mos amazing events in drag racing history — "The Last Drag Race.

Held on December 2, 1972, the last race ended an era tha can never be duplicated in drag racing, but to say Lions wen

Toward the end of the Lions Drag Strip era, the track switched from its former sanctioning body to the NHRA, under the leadership of new track manager, Steve Evans. With the end drawing near, signs were made for "The Last Drag Race" and the buzz throughout the drag racing industry made this a must-attend event. (Photo Courtesy Don Gillespie Collection)

Jeb Allen prepares for a blast down Lions Drag Strip during the last drag race. Allen fought his way through several rounds, and made it to the finals after being inserted back into the ladder after the Cerny & Moody fueler hurt an engine in the semi finals. Allen lost to Carl Olson in the finals. (Photo Courtesy Don Gillespie Collection)

The last drag race at Lions was an unforgettable event, and this final round featuring Snake versus Mongoose made it even better. More than 20,000 spectators invaded the track, forcing track manager Steve Evans to close the spectator gates at 6:00 pm. Countless people scaled the fences, determined to take part in the last event at Lions. (Photo Courtesy Don Gillespie Collection)

out with a bang would be a major understatement. Already expecting a big crowd, the track crew thought they were prepared, but more than 20,000 spectators made it an overwhelming experience. With virtually no control over the crowd, the track crew could only hope that no one would be seriously injured during the final event. Spectators scaled the fences to get a closer view of the races, and got an early start on the destruction of the track.

Racing went well into the night, with the spectators growing wilder as the minutes and hours ticked away. No one could prepare for the hilarity that ensued after the final round of eliminations, which saw Tom "Mongoose" McEwen outrun Don "The Snake" Prudhomme in an epic Funny Car battle. Later, it was Carl Olson getting past Jeb Allen in the Top Eliminator finals, which was ultimately the last drag race at Lions.

A truly sad sight, Lions Associated Drag Strip sits vacant shortly after it closed its doors in December 1972. The catwalk remained, as did the buildings, fences, and other structures, but the racing days were over. For eighteen years, Lions was the go-to track for drag racers across the country, but that didn't help it survive. (Photo Courtesy Don Gillespie Collection)

The Harbor Commission revoked its lease in order to take advantage of this piece of property, which ended a glorious era of drag racing. And while drag racing, as a sport, continued at other tracks, the fact that Lions was no longer on any racer's schedule provided a painful reality for everyone involved. (Photo Courtesy Don Gillespie Collection)

As the last pair blasted down the quarter mile, it was utter chaos as the massive crowd of spectators literally fought for pieces of memorabilia from the famed track. Signs, posters, and anything that could be removed were stripped from the track that very night. The 30-foot-long Lions Drag Strip sign was split into three pieces and hauled home by three groups of spectators, while the racers packed up their machines and waited for their final payout from Lions.

The closing of Lions Associated Drag Strip was heartbreaking to thousands of racers and spectators in the area, but if you missed out on "The Last Drag Race," you missed one of the wildest drag racing events in the history of the sport. There will never be another track like Lions, but we can reflect on all those good times, thanks to folks like Don Gillespie who have devoted countless hours collecting information, photographs, and videos from the legendary drag strip. Lions will never be forgotten.

Empty pits and parking lots made for an eerie feeling at Lions Drag Strip shortly after it closed. The property didn't remain vacant for long, as its prime location in Wilmington, just outside of Los Angeles, was a very valuable piece of industrial real estate. (Photo Courtesy Don Gillespie Collection)

The early days of OCIR can be seen in this shot of the pits. Killer tow vehicles and homemade enclosed trailers are enough to make modern-day hot rodders drool, but it was the race cars that garnered the most attention back then. How many cool station wagons can you spot? (Photo Courtesy Don Gillespie Collection)

Irvine, California
1967-1983

Current Status: ➤ **BUSINESS PARK**

In the mid 1960s, drag racing continued growing in popularity, evolving over the course of nearly two decades of its legitimate existence. Racers competed at high-brow events, and put on a great show, but marginal amenities for the competitors and spectators created the need for a "super track." Not an abandoned airfield or a low-budget operation, it was actually a high-class facility that offered the absolute best in terms of safety, spectator satisfaction, and racer appreciation. This facility was called Orange County International Raceway (OCIR).

Built in only six months, the high-tech track was state-of-the-art in every way, and it certainly wasn't a singular effort. Initially, Larry Vaughn, Bill White, Mike Jones, and Mike McKenna joined forces to create the concept and successfully obtained a fifty-five-year lease on a 113-acre piece of property in East Irvine where the Golden State and San Diego freeways met. The location offered easy access, but it also offered competition, as Lions and Irwindale were both a mere thirty minutes away. Mike Jones designed the track with high hopes of

ORANGE COUNTY INTERNATIONAL

RACEWAY

ORANGE COUNTY INTERNATIONAL RACEWAY IS LOCATED ON THE SANTA ANA FRWY 14 MI. SOUTH OF DISNEYLAND. EXIT THE SANTA ANA FRWY AT SAND CANYON AVE. OR EXIT THE SAN DIEGO FRWY AT VALENCIA AVE. CALL 714 838-3593

Orange County International Raceway (OCIR) was one of the sport's first mega-tracks, opening in 1967 with a total investment of nearly $750,000. With that kind of financial backing, the track was sure to be a spectacle in the drag racing world, and it certainly lived up to the hype. (Photo Courtesy Don Gillespie Collection)

luxury, and even though reality didn't quite meet his original expectation, it was certainly a step above any track of the time.

With the help of many investors and business partners, OCIR opened for its first event on August 5, 1967, and set out to take over the drag racing world with its ultra-plush environment. Spectators enjoyed spacious restrooms, clean concession stands, and perfectly positioned seating, while racers took advantage of a flawless racing surface with the utmost safety precautions. The track had an extremely long shutdown area, including a 300-foot sand trap in case a half mile wasn't enough. OCIR even had rollers, powered by a small-block Chevy engine, to start up the fuelers, which normally needed a push start. Total cost to build the track came close to $750,000.

There's nothing quite like the wow factor of two jet cars facing off! With fire, incredible noise, and blistering speeds, these exhibition cars were always a big hit. This shot offers a view of the OCIR timing tower, illuminated by fire from the Doug Rose *Green Mamba* jet car. (Photo Courtesy Don Gillespie Collection)

OCIR's seating gave spectators a great view of the action, while the distance from the racing surface provided a safe atmosphere when compared to other drag strips at the time. This mixture of safety and viewing pleasure kept spectators coming back to see the biggest events, which were typical (and year-round) for West Coast tracks. (Photo Courtesy Don Gillespie Collection)

Originally sanctioned by the NHRA, multiple changes in track management resulted in a five-year deal with the AHRA in 1973. Several managers ran the track through the early 1970s, including Bill Doner and Steve Evans. The track switched back to NHRA sanctioning, with former racer Charlie Allen taking over operations. A major renovation brought the track back to life, and some say that the best years of OCIR were under Charlie Allen's management. Huge events, such as the "64 funny cars" events, brought in thousands of spectators on a regular basis, but rising taxes and fees made deep cuts into the profit margin.

OCIR was home of big Funny Car events, as well as numerous national events. The track was sanctioned by both the NHRA and the AHRA through the years, so OCIR saw plenty of action in its sixteen years of operation, such as this run by Billy Meyer. A big investment turned into quite the profit center, with huge crowds visiting the track several times per year. (Photo Courtesy Don Gillespie Collection)

The timing tower at OCIR is one of the most memorable aspects of the high-dollar drag strip, providing a great backdrop for many incredible pictures, such as this nighttime shot of Don Prudhomme. With the candles lit and the tower in the background, the moment is perfectly captured. (Photo Courtesy Don Gillespie Collection)

Another problem was the increase in property development surrounding the OCIR grounds—the end was near. As each year passed, the property owners realized how much the 113-acre piece of property was worth, so the group pushed to take over the property and develop it. Desperate to keep the track alive, one of OCIR's original team members, Larry Vaughn, was able to squeeze another few years out of the property. The sad fact was that OCIR was the last remaining drag strip in Southern California, as all of the other greats had been closed for various reasons. Lions, Irwindale, Fontana, San Fernando, San Gabriel—they were all gone.

In October 1983, it happened. The last drag race was held, and just as Lions had done more than a decade prior, OCIR went out with a bang. A capacity crowd stayed until 3:00 am to watch the finals, which saw Gary Beck take the win in Top

A sign that no one wanted to see—the last drag race. In October 1983, OCIR held its final event, which drew racers and spectators from thousands of miles away. This big event didn't mark the official end of OCIR, as it held a smaller, low-key event the following weekend for its regular weekend racers. (Photo Courtesy Don Gillespie Collection)

This shot shows the landscape of the track, and its vast distance between the racing surface and the bleachers. This was uncommon in drag racing when OCIR was first built in 1967, as spectators were accustomed to being on top of the action. It became the standard for all major tracks due to safety concerns. (Photo Courtesy Don Gillespie Collection)

Just like the last drag race at Lions, the final big event at OCIR filled the place to capacity. The majority of the crowd stayed until 3:00 am to watch the final rounds, which pitted the nation's biggest names against each other in a fitting end to an amazing Southern California drag strip. (Photo Courtesy Don Gillespie Collection)

With its guardrails, bleachers, and timing equipment stripped, OCIR sat vacant shortly after its final event in 1983. The track's final manager, Charlie Allen, utilized these components when building Firebird International Raceway in Chandler, Arizona, leaving behind only a strip of pavement and the unforgettable OCIR timing tower. (Photo Courtesy Don Gillespie Collection)

The tower didn't get much respect from the locals, as this photo reveals its broken windows. OCIR sat vacant for a few months while the surrounding land was developed, but this property was far too valuable to remain untouched. It is now filled with buildings, showing no remnants of the legendary track. (Photo Courtesy Don Gillespie Collection)

After closing in 1983, OCIR was yet another track added to an ever-growing list of SoCal drag strips that were no longer in operation. All the greats—Lions, Santa Ana, Riverside—were eventually gone, with no hope of new tracks coming into the picture. Even the longstanding LA County Raceway (LACR), located far away from Los Angeles in Palmdale, California, eventually succumbed to outside pressures and closed in 2007. (Photo Courtesy Don Gillespie Collection)

Fuel and Kenny Bernstein take the Funny Car victory in the professional classes. A huge field of bracket racers also turned out for the final event.

What many people don't know is that the "last drag race" wasn't technically the last race at OCIR. The following Saturday was the real last race, but it was a low-key event compared to the week before. It gave local racers a chance to sit back and enjoy their last time at the track, and reminisce about the good times and the bad times that OCIR had brought into their lives. It was a sad goodbye, as the "super track" fell victim to Southern California's ultimate urbanization.

The track's final operator, Charlie Allen went on to build Firebird International Raceway in Arizona, where he used many components from OCIR. Sitting unoccupied for months, the track was stripped of its grandstands, timing equipment, and anything deemed usable. What was once a state-of-the-art timing tower stood alone in a vast, empty expanse of property, which was later filled with various businesses. The only thing left from the legendary track is the Sand Canyon Avenue gate, but it offers very little nostalgic value, considering the scope of what will always be referred to as the first super track in the world of drag racing.

The crudely painted message on the door says it all. Even if you never set foot on the OCIR property, this picture is a sad reminder that even the best drag strips couldn't survive the rapid urbanization of Southern California. By the mid 1980s, drag racing had hit an all-time low with multiple track closures. (Photo Courtesy Don Gillespie Collection)

The only part of OCIR's property that wasn't heavily developed is this small area, surrounded by chain-link fencing. This was the original sand trap at the end of the strip, although it doesn't look like much today. (Photo Courtesy David Giles)

Riverside International Raceway was the ultimate multi-tasking race facility, with possibilities for road course racing, oval racing, and drag racing, all crammed into one beautiful track. According to the Riverside International Automotive Museum, the drag strip was being worked into the existing track as early as June 1958. (Photo Courtesy Riverside International Automotive Museum and Petersen Automotive Museum)

Riverside, California
1959–1970 and 1983–1986

Current Status: ➤ SHOPPING MALL

While the other tracks in this chapter served strictly as drag strips, a facility known as Riverside International Raceway had many more uses. In fact, it was more popular for its road course, which played host to NASCAR, Formula One, and multiple Indy Car events. The idea of a multi-use race track was ingenious because it allowed anyone with an interest in automobiles to partake in the fun, instead of catering to one specific niche of the hobby. As we all know, NASCAR fans aren't necessarily drag racing fans, and vice versa, so the broad appeal of Riverside International Raceway made for a very profitable business.

The track, originally known as Riverside International Motor Raceway, had been proposed in the mid 1950s, and obviously took a bit more effort to construct than a standard drag strip, due to its complex road course. Even so, it took less than a year from start to finish to build. Riverside's road course had a total length of 3.3 miles, made up of nine turns and a 1.1-mile straightaway. It didn't take much consideration to turn the back stretch into a drag strip, as it had plenty of length, plenty of width, and a smooth surface.

The first recorded race at Riverside occurred in September 1957, but it wasn't a drag race—instead it was a California Sports Car Club road race event. Drag racing at Riverside didn't begin until 1959, and further track development resulted in a small asphalt oval, which utilized a portion of the road course. It was truly a motorsports park.

In terms of drag racing, the Riverside facility was a popular place. It had all the makings of a professionally sanctioned

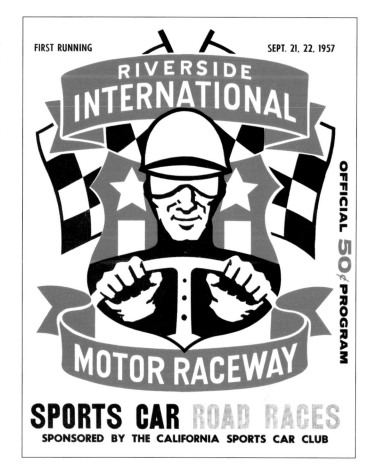

When it officially opened in 1957, Riverside International Motor Raceway was primarily used for its road course. It held its first major event on September 21 and 22, 1957, a road race event sanctioned by the California Sports Car Club. Riverside later incorporated a drag strip and oval track into its layout. (Photo Courtesy Riverside International Automotive Museum and Petersen Automotive Museum)

Marvin Schwartz hazes the tires in his immaculate AA/FD as he leaves the line at Riverside. The track went through a few different phases, but it was certainly the most popular in the mid to late 1960s. Western drag strips tended to draw a considerable number of dragsters, compared to other parts of the country. (Photo Courtesy Don Gillespie Collection)

drag strip, and it was certainly in a nice location for spectator accessibility. And though C. J. "Pappy" Hart of Santa Ana Drag Strip fame had already set the standard length of drag racing to a quarter mile nearly a decade prior, it was decided that Riverside would hold half-mile drags on its extremely long strip. These half-mile events were not sanctioned by the NHRA or any other drag racing organization. The events were put on by the SCTA, the same group that raced regularly on the salt flats and dry lake beds. Because of unfit track conditions, the land speed racers ran at Riverside during what they considered the off-season. Regular drag racers joined in the fun, but the SCTA Half Mile Drags were geared toward land speed cars and lasted for only a few years in the early to mid 1960s.

Standard quarter-mile drag racing at Riverside consisted of the normal West Coast crowd, with big-name fuel cars making up a large portion of the wow factor. The NHRA held

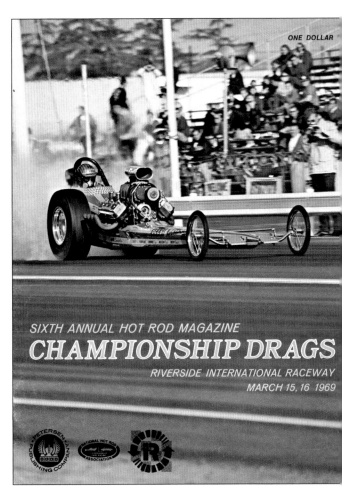

SIXTH ANNUAL HOT ROD MAGAZINE
CHAMPIONSHIP DRAGS
RIVERSIDE INTERNATIONAL RACEWAY
MARCH 15, 16 1969

ONE DOLLAR

Although it was home to many big events, Riverside's drag racing era is best known for being the home of the Hot Rod Magazine Championship Drags. These events, which were supported by the NHRA, were always a big deal, with the nation's top names doing battle. The Hot Rod Magazine Championship Drags lasted from 1964 to 1969. (Photo Courtesy Riverside International Automotive Museum and Petersen Automotive Museum)

In this fantastic shot of Gas Ronda's Mustang funny car battling an injected dragster in the far lane, you can see th Riverside timing tower in the background. It's also a great stop-action shot as the blown funny car wrinkles its Goodye. Blue Streak slicks off the line. (Photo Courtesy Don Gillespie Collection)

Riverside had a long racing surface, and even hosted the SCTA Half Mile Drags in the 1960s. Here a pair of dragsters comes to a halt with the assistance of parachutes. In the upper right corner of the frame, you can see the catwalk, which made an interesting vantage point. (Photo Courtesy Riverside International Automotive Museum and Petersen Automotive Museum)

During drag racing events, racers and spectators filled Riverside's huge facility. The track had its most successful seasons under the management of former pro football player Les Richter, who ran Riverside from 1963 to 1983. The track only lasted a few more years after he left. (Photo Courtesy Riverside International Automotive Museum and Petersen Automotive Museum)

regional races at Riverside in the 1960s, but in terms of drag racing, the track may be best remembered for the Hot Rod Magazine Championship Drags, held from 1964 to 1969—what many consider the heyday of drag racing. The Hot Rod Drags had huge sponsorships with very healthy payouts and prizes, so it drew large crowds of racers, which inherently drew large numbers of spectators. These sponsored races were the idea of *Hot Rod* staffers, Bob Greene and Ray Brock, who worked closely with Wally Parks to create an event that very much mimicked an NHRA national points meet. In fact, the NHRA timed the event, and honored any records set during the events, so it was a legitimate deal.

Riverside underwent major changes in the late 1960s and into the 1970s. The back stretch and adjacent turns were reconfigured to make the road course safer by reducing the speeds possible on the back stretch. This put the drag strip out of commission for some time, and it wasn't in the best interest of the track to continue holding drag racing events, so Riverside concentrated on its bread and butter (the road course) for several years after the end of drag racing. Nearly fifteen years later, the track again featured drag racing, but for the most part, the thrill was gone.

In general, the track had the most success under the leadership of former NFL player, Les Richter. Highly respected in the racing world, Richter ran the Riverside facility from 196[?] until 1983, before handing over the keys to new owner Frit[z] Duda. During this time, the drag strip was brought back to lif[e] for the final five years of its existence. Drag races were hel[d] until the track's last season, but it didn't cater to the big dog[s] as in the old days. The modern era of drag racing at Riversid[e] was best suited for street cars and mild drag cars, rather tha[n] all-out fuel cars, which ran there on a regular basis in the 1960[s].

As the SoCal population continued to grow, the track['s] owner realized the value of his property and closed Riversid[e] International Raceway in 1989. The final major race was hel[d] in 1988, but the doors were officially closed the followin[g] year. The first new structure to be built on the property wa[s] the Moreno Valley Mall, which was completed in 1992. Nex[t] houses filled the southern portion of the track, while othe[r] areas remained untouched for a few more years.

Today, there's nothing left of the old track, aside from th[e] fond memories of each racer who laid rubber on the famou[s] asphalt. Unfortunately, it's not even recognizable, as the land[-]scape has changed dramatically, but it will forever remain a[s] one of the greatest racing facilities of all time, thanks to it[s] versatility, location, and solid management.

After it shut down in the late 1980s, portions of Riversid[e] International Raceway remained untouched for sever[al] years. The first new structure to be built on the propert[y] was the Moreno Valley Mall in 1992, with more building[s] and houses built soon thereafter. Here, the old building[s] are still standing. (Photo Courtesy Don Gillespie Collectio[n])

With the catwalk still intact, the shutdown area is unde[r] going its destruction. The track remained in operatio[n] until 1989, when its owner, Fritz Duda, decided it was tim[e] to sell the highly valued real estate. It was an unfortunat[e] end to a long-running track that catered to a wide varie[ty] of racers. (Photo Courtesy Don Gillespie Collection)

BEE LINE DRAGWAY

Bee Line Dragway was built in 1963 on a flat piece of desert property owned by the Salt River Pima-Maricopa Indian Community. Richard Petty is seen here in his infamous *Outlawed* Barracuda, facing off against Dick Harrell in the first running of the Factory Experimental class, held at the 1965 AHRA Winter Nationals. (Photo Courtesy John Durand)

Mesa, Arizona
1963–1980

Current Status: ➤ **ABANDONED**

Of the four drag strips featured in this chapter, Bee Line Dragway most perfectly embodies the true spirit of an abandoned drag strip—a ghost track if you will. It's still in the middle of the desert, but the noise of drag racing is long gone, making for an eerie feeling, as the dust blows across the ground, essentially burying the weathered racing surface with loose sand.

Originally built in 1963, Bee Line Dragway offered a convenient place to race for many gearheads in the Mesa,

Tempe, Phoenix, and Scottsdale area. It was approximately twenty minutes northeast of Phoenix, and was located in an unpopulated area with very little civilization in sight. The wide-open space of the East Valley didn't have the same "in your backyard" feeling as many of the other tracks, and that had its good points and bad points. Situated on the Salt River Pima-Maricopa Indian Community, Bee Line was built and managed by Jim Rodgers, who was part of a team of investors. Rodgers found the property and obtained a lease from

This shot of Don Schumacher's Vega funny car also offers partial views of the track's massive timing tower and catwall. The timing tower was a new addition to the track for the 1972 season, even though the previous tower was considered top-of-the-line when it was built in 1963. (Photo Courtesy Don Gillespie Collection)

Another classic funny car shot, this time of the *Sun Devil Hustler* Mustang, also shows off a fresh paint job on the tower, which was necessary due to its change to NHRA sanctioning in the mid 1970s. Toward the end of the Bee Line era, other sponsor logos were painted on the tower. (Photo Courtesy Bob Snyder)

the Native American community, then laid the foundation for what eventually became a world-class drag racing facility. Bee Line Dragway opened in 1963 and wasted little time bagging a major event, the AHRA Winter Nationals, held in February 1964.

During the development of Bee Line, the main objective was safety, as many of the drag strips had earned bad reputations because of poor safety precautions. Bee Line was an extraordinary track that not only kept the safety of spectators in mind, but also that of the drivers, who put their life at risk every time they strapped into the cockpit.

For crowd safety, a 3-foot-high concrete safety barrier separated the racing surface from the spectator area. And for the drivers, the strip of pavement was 60 feet wide and 3/4 mile in length, with another 1/4 mile of runoff area, in the case of throttle hang-ups and 'chute malfunctions. Even if you couldn't get stopped in the provided mile of pavement, there was literally no structure in sight, so the worries of running out of room were all but gone when racing at Bee Line.

With an initial investment of $125,000 to build the track, it was a top-of-the-line facility, with a glass-enclosed, three-story timing tower and a purpose-built timing system from Chrondek. Racer convenience was also considered during the development of Bee Line, with fully paved pits making life a lot easier for the drivers and the crews, no matter what class they raced.

According to an article in the November 1963 issue of *Drag News* magazine, Jim Rodgers worked as track manager, while a team of investors helped run the business side of Bee Line. The team consisted of President Tim Rodgers, Vice President Archie Campbell, Secretary William Orr, and Treasurer George Podd, none of whom had any prior drag racing experience, but had plenty of business knowledge. Without question, the track was a big hit, with its high level of details, central location, and extreme safety precautions.

In the pits and spectator areas, concession stands offered food and refreshments, while permanent restrooms added to the convenience factor. A quality PA system with numerous speakers throughout the pits helped racers to hear necessary announcements, such as being called to the staging lanes, which ultimately meant less downtime for the fans. Parking space was virtually unlimited, and Bee Line offered a lot of spectator seating for large events. The track also committed to having emergency vehicles and tow trucks on hand at all times, in case of an accident on the grounds. Many of these details were not yet established at most drag strips, making Bee Line a great place for national meets.

In the beginning, Bee Line was sanctioned by the AHRA, which was a huge competitor to the NHRA sanctioning body. Different rule sets, class structures, and drag strips separated the two organizations, and during the early to mid 1960s,

Although it's hard not to notice the wild ride occurring on the track, this classic photo shows the general landscape of the track. With a very wide racing surface, and wide strips of grass between the track and safety barriers, Bee Line gave racers a bit of wiggle room if things got out of hand. (Photo Courtesy Don Gillespie Collection)

Top Fuel racer Mike Wagoner is seen here making a pass at Bee Line Dragway at the 1974 AHRA Winter Nationals. During the AHRA era, the track was home to the first points meet of the year, and later went on to host the NHRA season opener known as the Winter Classic. (Photo Courtesy Don Gillespie Collection)

AHRA made a name for itself by allowing nitromethane during the infamous NHRA "fuel ban." While the AHRA sanctioned numerous small tracks across the country, it made big moves in the industry by making deals with new, high-tech tracks.

As mentioned earlier, Bee Line was selected as home of the AHRA Winter Nationals in February 1964, and continued to host the event until 1974. The second year of the Winter Nationals at Bee Line marked a huge breakthrough in drag racing, as the AHRA set aside a specific class for factory experimental, altered-wheelbase cars, which later became known as A/FX, and then Funny Car.

Through the years, the track remained a drag racing staple in the Phoenix area, and underwent major renovation during the early 1970s. By 1972, the track had a brand-new timing tower, this time much larger and positioned on the opposite side of the track. The huge tower remained unpainted, showing its bare cinder blocks for some time, but was eventually painted to incorporate Winston logos, a major sponsor at the time. As time went on, the track changed to NHRA sanctioning, holding events such as the NHRA Winter Classic, the season opener. The AHRA moved its Winter Nationals event to Tucson, Arizona.

After seventeen years of successful operation and many national events from various sanctioning bodies, a disagreement between track management and the land owners spelled the end of Bee Line Dragway. The Native American Community reclaimed the land, but had no intention of reopening the drag strip. Redevelopment of the property wasn't part of the plan either—the owners of the property simply abandoned it.

After the Salt River Pima-Maricopa Indian Community revoked the lease on Bee Line Dragway, the property sat vacant. Measures were taken to ensure no one raced on the abandoned strip, which has now disintegrated, due to abuse from the the blowing sand and extreme sun. It's a sad sight for these hallowed grounds to be covered with sand. (Photo Courtesy Don Gillespie Collection)

Through all the drama during the track's closure, the tower st
stands. It has been vandalized severely, but now serves a
somewhat of a historic monument to a wonderful Western trac
The tower has been stripped of all scrap metal, and it no longe
has any windows. (Photo Courtesy Don Gillespie Collection)

The tower is still standing, but little remains of the racing surface and pits, after more than thirty years of neglect. Large portions of the track were dug up to prevent passersby from making an illegal pass down the deserted strip, and there is now a fence blocking any outsiders from vandalizing the forgotten tower, even though it is covered in graffiti. Although faded, you can still see the Winston logo, as well as various local sponsors, such as Saguaro Automotive. The bleachers are gone, the concrete barriers are gone, and the catwalk is gone . . . just a lonely timing tower remains to tell the story of a track that saw lots of amazing moments and provided nearly twenty years of drag racing action to the greater Phoenix area.

Nearly all of the paint has faded from the block building, but you can still make out the Winston logo (toward the ground), as well as the Saguaro Automotive logo (at the top). Bee Line Dragway operated successfully for seventeen years, and has sat vacant for more than thirty years. A disagreement between the land owners and track operators killed it in 1980. (Photo Courtesy Don Gillespie Collection)

CHAPTER 4

SOMEWHERE IN THE MIDDLE

There are folks who say hot rodding originated on the West Coast, and while those folks have a good point, it doesn't mean gearheads in other parts of the country didn't have a few ideas of their own. Drag racing certainly had its hotspot in Southern California, but other states had plenty to offer as well.

As we move eastward on the map, this chapter focuses on tracks located in the Midwest. While not as centralized as the West Coast drag racing scene, Midwest drag strips were quite popular with local racers and spectators, and offered lots of variety. The mostly flat landscape of the Midwest promoted the building of drag strips, as it required minimal ground work, and after all, that is the most important part of a drag strip, right? Owners soon learned that timing equipment, spectator amenities, and racer conveniences cost the most, but in the early days, Midwest drag strips were hardly more than a strip of pavement on a vacant piece of farmland, so none of those factors came into play.

Although simple by nature, Midwestern tracks eventually caught up in terms of creature comforts. Bigger restrooms, timing towers, and safety equipment brought the tracks up to date, and new classes kept the action interesting year in and year out.

Whether talking about the racing surface, the general atmosphere, or the racers, each track had its good points and bad points, but all four tracks in this chaper allowed racers to do what they do. In the end, that's all that matters, regardless of the reason for closing the doors.

Most of the tracks featured in this chapter were sanctioned by the AHRA, which was a heavy-hitting sanctioning body, and the NHRA's only real competition until the IHRA stepped into the picture in the early 1970s. With Midwest

A dragster being slowed to a stop by a parachute is a beautiful sight, but there's just something cool about doing it in the middle of a field, as here at Oswego. That was the joy of Midwest drag racing in the 1950s and 1960s. The naturally flat landscape was perfect for farming, and even better for drag racing. (Photo Courtesy Brent Fregin)

Dave Billingsley is seen here launching hard at Motion Raceway. His 1967 Camaro is a perfect example of a Midwestern drag car from the 1970s. It had all the cool stuff—Centerline wheels, Firestone slicks, a square-snorkel hood scoop, and a funky paint job. The Midwest was doorslammer heaven in the 1970s. (Photo Courtesy Steve Jackson)

Drag racing was hot in the late 1960s and early 1970s, and it wasn't just the West Coast guys who had all the fun. Midwestern drag strips were packed with action during the sport's heyday, as evidenced by this pit shot taken at Oswego Dragway. Altered roadsters, stock-class street cars, and everything in between made for a diverse field of racers. (Photo Courtesy Brent Fregin)

track owner and promoter Ben Christ having a large stake in the AHRA, all of his tracks were AHRA-sanctioned until a falling out in the late 1970s.

Many Midwestern tracks opened in the late 1950s and early 1960s, but the next two decades were not kind to the area and its drag strips. Several Michigan tracks closed in 1978, and Oswego Dragway in Illinois shut down the following year. Many others closed in the early 1980s, especially after the AHRA shut down for good in 1984, leaving many tracks without a sanctioning body. A tough economy, increased population, and blossoming noise ordinances caused much of the dismay for drag racing enthusiasts, and it was a losing battle for racers to go up against the local governments.

There has always been a glimmer of hope for many of the tracks featured in this chapter to be revitalized, but through various ownership and governmental changes, progress has been minimal.

The Midwest is a large region of the country with numerous remaining drag strips, but the ratio of closing tracks to brand-new tracks is certainly unbalanced. Historic racing facilities are closing at an alarming rate, due to the same reasons drag strips closed in the 1970s and 1980s. A poor economy and expanding communities are still almost always the culprits for the closure of these rural area tracks.

A big Midwest track that saw unfortunate times is Gateway International Raceway in Madison, Illinois. Its oval track was NASCAR sanctioned, its quarter-mile drag strip was NHRA sanctioned, and it had a great infield road course, but that didn't stop the owners from nearly killing it. Dover Motorsports Inc. owned the property and decided to pull the plug after losing profits on the facility. In late 2010, it was announced that the track would be closed indefinitely. However, after no events in 2011, the track reopened for the 2012 season, under a short-term lease agreement made by Curtis Francois.

The fear of losing your local drag strip is all too real, and it happens all the time. For the Midwest racing crowd, it seems to happen in spurts, but hopefully it doesn't become a common occurrence. The Midwest has always had cool drag strips, and the region is packed with car guys, so regardless of the recent politics involving several tracks, it should remain a great place to race for years to come. For the less fortunate facilities that didn't stand the test of time, it's important to keep the memories alive and pay respect to these historic Midwest drag strips.

The harsh reality of drag racing is that it suffered greatly in the late 1970s and early 1980s. Many tracks closed, which left many of them to deteriorate beyond repair. One such example is Motor City Dragway, which is located in New Baltimore, Michigan. Once a very popular track, it is now nothing more than a memory. (Photo Courtesy www.waterwinterwonderland.com)

MOTION RACEWAY

From behind the burnout box, you really get an idea of the extremely flat landscape of Motion Raceway. The actual racing surface was very wide, giving racers plenty of room to do their thing. Speaking of which, Gerald Edwards in his Mopar and Bob Kimbro in his Nova are doing just that, while Earl Hendricks in his GTO waits his turn. (Photo Courtesy Steve Jackson)

Assumption, Illinois 1970-1983

Current Status: ➤ ABANDONED

While many of the drag strip features in this book involve tracks that were built in the early days of the sport, Motion Raceway tells a different story of the evolution of drag racing. There is little doubt that increasing safety precautions, outrageous insurance prices, and a slightly dwindling crowd discouraged folks from building new drag strips during the 1970s, but it seemed to have been a good move for this Midwestern track, located in Assumption, Illinois. Positioned near the center of the state, Motion Raceway catered to a number of racers in the surrounding counties, and offered more than a decade of exciting action for racers and spectators.

You'll quickly notice that Motion Raceway was never intended to be a mega track. However, to the folks who raced here every weekend, it was as good as drag racing could get.

The rural location didn't keep it from attracting big names from time to time, including Ronnie Sox, who occasionally rented the track for testing during the week. Special events also drew lots of well-known racers to the track, which was surrounded by farmland.

The man behind the drag strip is John Jones. A car guy and former street racer, Jones owned a sizable piece of land just outside Assumption. Fresh out of the military, John wanted to provide a safe place to race, so he decided to build a drag strip on his property. It was a flat piece of land requiring very little preliminary work to be ready for a fresh strip of pavement. The original plan was to have a coin-operated gate, making the track available to racers at any time. This was a perfect scenario for street racers, as it offered a safe place to race, without the risk of getting in trouble with the local law

Another typical Midwest doorslammer, this Ford Maverick puts the racing surface to the ultimate test. Motion Raceway opened in 1970, putting it a bit later in the game than some tracks, but that didn't stop it from being a popular track for folks in central Illinois. (Photo Courtesy Steve Jackson)

Wayne Wells campaigned this Plymouth Barracuda, which was a favorite for the Mopar crowd at Motion Raceway in Assumption, Illinois. Although the track was built as a conventional drag strip, the initial idea for Motion Raceway involved a coin-operated gate, which gave racers the freedom to come and go as they pleased. (Photo Courtesy Steve Jackson)

Although many drag racers shifted focus from dragsters to door cars in the 1970s, the old-style rail jobs were still popular with spectators. Here, the supercharged small-block Chevy-powered dragster in the near lane has a tough opponent in *Overtime*, Lee Stewart's injected Fiat altered in the far lane. (Photo Courtesy Steve Jackson)

his nighttime shot of Delbert and Janice Melton's *Thunder & Lightning* Camaro provides a glimpse of the Motion Race-
ay timing tower, which was considered state-of-the-art in its day. When the track shut down in 1983, the facility was
ismantled and the tower was moved to nearby Macon Speedway. (Photo Courtesy Steve Jackson)

Everyone loves a jet-car match race, so drag strip operators often invited these exhibition vehicles to draw in large crowds. The ultimate wow factor comes when these jet-powered dragsters bump into the staging beams and leave the line. Lee Shockley's aptly named *Shock Wave* dragster is seen here at Motion Raceway. (Photo Courtesy Steve Jackson)

Now here's an interesting matchup that you probably wouldn't see today because of the countless safety regulations it violates. You have Jim Strobel in his *Super Star* funny car, lined up against what looks like a stock street bike in the far lane. (Photo Courtesy Steve Jackson)

Abandoned for thirty years, the old Motion Raceway doesn't have much to offer besides a massive strip of cracked pavement. Usually, when tracks close down, many of the components are reused at other tracks or sold for scrap, leaving a lonely strip of pavement as the only reminder of a great track. (Photo Courtesy Steve Jackson)

enforcement. As Jones continued to ponder the possibilities, he visited other drag strips to get ideas.

Jones surveyed the land himself, and drew up the plans for the drag strip. Long gone was the idea for a coin-operated gate—Motion Raceway was a full-fledged drag strip. During the planning stages, Jones also considered building an oval track next to the drag strip, but the idea never materialized. Jones had a 3,000-foot expanse of asphalt laid on his property in 1970, and outfitted the facility with guardrails, bleachers, a timing tower, and other buildings. Jones went the extra mile to cater to his racers, installing rollers for the cars that required push-starting, which was certainly considered a luxury by most racers. The rollers opened the door for fuel dragsters and funny cars to run at Motion Raceway, which always attracted a big crowd.

Finished in late 1970, the track's first official event wa held in early 1971. Jones sought help from his brother, Pau and the two successfully ran the track until 1979. With a entry fee of $6 for a car and its driver, Motion Raceway wa a budget-friendly drag strip with a great surface and racin program. Although many of the tracks featured in this boo opened much earlier than this Illinois drag strip, it landed in great era of drag racing.

During the early 1970s, the development of Modifie Eliminator, Pro Stock, and many other classes made fo diverse fields of cars, and match races were always welcome as well. Other attractions, such as the always popular exhibi tion cars, made Motion Raceway a favorite for many spec tators. Bill "Maverick" Golden attended the track with hi

the distance is the remains of the concession stand at Motion Raceway. It's certainly seen better days, much like the est of the old track. The guardrails are long gone, as are the bleachers and other buildings. This is what thirty years of eglect looks like. (Photo Courtesy Steve Jackson)

ittle Red Wagon, as did many other wheelstanders of the era. et cars were also a big hit at Motion, with big names such as ee Shockley and Art Arfons making ferocious passes down he quarter-mile.

Motion Raceway was eventually converted from a full uarter-mile track to 1,000 feet for safety purposes, but the icers adapted and continued to support the track. From 1980 its final season in 1983, Jones ran the track without the ssistance of his brother, and kept his program fairly simple. t the end of the 1983 racing season, rumors swirled about the ontinuation of the track, but due to several conflicts, Jones osed the doors for good. According to local sources, there ere often rumors that the track would reopen, but it never aterialized.

When Motion Raceway closed, the stands were torn down and hauled away, as was the in-ground roll starter, but the timing tower lived to fight another day. It was actually moved to nearby Macon Speedway in Macon, Illinois.

Until 2008, the property was used for grain storage by a local farmers' co-op, and when it was no longer used for storage, there was once again a slight glimmer of hope for racing at Motion. Greg Clayton of New Covenant Performance made big plans to rejuvenate the track, allowing for street-style racing to take place on the once-abandoned track. His plans involved low-key, run-for-fun drag racing, but it would certainly be a wake-up call to the property, which hadn't seen any real action since 1983. Unfortunately, the plans fell through and the strip of pavement continues to sit unused.

MOTOR CITY DRAGWAY

Unlike many of the tracks featured in this book, Motor City Raceway still has most of its buildings. Although in very poor condition, the buildings are still there and the racing surface remains intact. Having closed in 1978, the asphalt is almost completely consumed by weeds. (Photo Courtesy www.waterwinterwonderland.com)

New Baltimore, Michigan
1957–1978

Current Status: ➤ **ABANDONED**

While the West Coast's hot rodding crowd thrived during the 1950s, it wasn't the only part of the country that had the fever. The Midwest, especially the Detroit area, was a hotspot for fast cars, and that led to the founding of the Michigan Hot Rod Association (MHRA) in 1951. Multiple Detroit-area car clubs made up the MHRA, with the number growing each year. By the mid 1950s, the MHRA boasted participation from more than forty car clubs. The group organized and promoted

the Detroit Autorama Rod and Custom Car Show in 1953, which continues to be one of the largest indoor car show spectacles each year.

During the early days of the MHRA, there were no official drag strips, although the formation of the group certainly encouraged young car guys to meet up with other young car guys, which can only result in one thing—racing. Informal drag racing started soon after the MHRA was founded, and it was 1954 before it was legitimized to a certain degree.

With bright yellow paint and nicely painted lettering, the Motor City Dragway signage always stood out well in photographs. This amazing shot provides a nice view of the racing surface, as well as the very close bleacher location, which offered a great view of the action! (Photo Courtesy JoeStevensPhotos.com)

This photograph shows Norm Lupo's 1956 Chevy leaving the line in a fury. The '56 Bel Air hardtop is a nice example of a 1960s-style drag car, and this photo does a great job of showing the surroundings of the track. Behind the racing surface was a farm house and barn. (Photo Courtesy JoeStevensPhotos.com)

The MHRA received permission from the city of Livonia to drag race on a newly paved section of Amrhein Road, just behind a new General Motors manufacturing facility. It was a big deal for the Detroit area, and the NHRA quickly jumped on board to support the drag strip in Livonia. It was a 3/4-mile strip of brand-new concrete, and it was perfect for drag racing. Unfortunately, racing in Livonia didn't last, so the next step was to try the Michigan State Fairgrounds as a new venue. That didn't work out either, so the group pressed on to find a solution for their drag racing needs.

With money raised from the Autorama and MHRA members, the group put a down payment on a piece of property on Meldrum Road in New Baltimore, Michigan. For more than a year, MHRA members spent evenings and weekends working on the property to get it ready for action. The members did nearly everything themselves, trying to save as much money as possible. The finished product made its debut in May 1957 after thousands of man hours and MHRA-raised dollars.

Through the years, the track enjoyed lots of success as it proved to be a major attraction to Detroit car guys, even if they were not associated with the growing MHRA. Bob Larivee was an MHRA Board Member and he had also been the manager of the drag strip before he moved on to promoting the Autorama. Later, Al Dortenzio managed the track, and then MHRA President (and the track's former flagman) Lee Lasky took a stab at the management side of drag-strip life.

During the track's early years, it had a fully pneumatic timing system, consisting of air hoses that ran across the racing surface. Originally, there was only a hose at the start line and finish line, but they later added a hose to calculate the speed of the vehicle. The timing system certainly wasn't state-of-the-art, and the unpaved pits didn't offer the cleanest environment, but the track served its purpose.

A few short years after the track opened, the MHRA began running eighth-mile drags, but racing eventually went back to a full quarter mile by the 1960s.

Although it was originally known as MHRA Drag Strip, the name eventually changed to Motor City Dragway, which is how many folks in the area remember it. As the drag racing scene grew rapidly in the 1960s, the wow factor of Motor City Dragway decreased, which led the MHRA Board of Directors to sell the property and get out of the drag racing business. Gil Kohn purchased the property and the business in 1961, adding it to a list of tracks that he owned and operated during his drag racing days. Kohn also owned Detroit Dragway, competing drag strip on the other side of town.

Both of these Detroit-area drag strips offered great events on a regular basis and provided car manufacturers with a nice place to test their vehicles. Modern timing equipment and a good racing surface meant auto manufacturers got the very best out of their new machines. Motor City Dragway saw its share of fame with several major magazine covers. The most popular was the December 1965 *Car Craft* magazine cover, featuring Pontiac's new 1966 GTO, which had the famous Motor City Dragway timing tower in the background.

Roger Lindamood's *Color Me Gone* funny car is seen here performing a dry hop at Motor City Dragway. Funny cars were huge attractions at nearly every drag strip in America during the 1960s, but Motor City also had a great dragster following, along with the exciting Super Stockers craze during the mid-1960s and into the 1970s. (Photo Courtesy JoeStevensPhotos.com)

Another view of the *Color Me Gone* Dodge Charger shows Roger Lindamood applying a little more throttle than the photo at left. This test pass was in preparation for a match race with Terry Hedrick and his popular *Seaton's Super Shaker* funny car. This sort of action is what kept the sport alive during some of the tough times. (Photo Courtesy JoeStevensPhotos.com)

Although wildly popular for quite some time, Motor City Dragway had to deal with the abundance of drag strips in the Detroit area, but that didn't cause its ultimate demise. Township ordinances regarding noise were the major blow that knocked Motor City off its feet, and the fast-spreading population didn't help matters. It is rumored that attendance and racer participation was also down because of a fish fly infestation in the area. When the track closed, there was no hope to reopen it, as the noise was far too much for local residents, even though the track was in place long before the new houses.

The closure of Motor City Dragway meant that local drag racers had to resort to other area tracks, making it nothing but a memory. Making matters even worse for Michigan drag racers, nearby Tri-City Dragway and Onondaga Dragway also closed in 1978, bringing an end to the days of drag strip barnstorming in the area.

Here Terry Hedrick is getting a little out of shape on what appears to be a crazy burnout. This shot also shows more of the surroundings of the track, including more farm equipment, such as the barn and grain silo in the background. (Photo Courtesy JoeStevensPhotos.com)

Many of the buildings were not even built when the track was initially opened by the Michigan Hot Rod Association in 1957. The yellow paint is a reminder of this once vibrant drag strip that hasn't been active in more than three decades. (Photo Courtesy www.waterwinter wonderland.com)

Yet another old building is still standing but in poor shape. Motor City Dragway had numerous buildings on site, all of which remain on the property, although most of them are on the verge of falling down. Years of neglect have taken a toll on the old drag strip. (Photo Courtesy www.waterwinterwonderland.com)

Built of cinder block, this building is still standing firm, but its roof has rotted substantially. This was a concession stand, and you can tell it was built in a different era than most of the other buildings, which were made of wood and painted bright yellow. (Photo Courtesy www.waterwinterwonderland.com)

Inside the concession stand, you can see that the wiring has been stripped away, and vandalism has been a recurring problem. With all of the wooden buildings on the property, it's amazing that they didn't get burned or torn down at some point over the years. (Photo Courtesy www.waterwinterwonderland.com)

The first level of the timing tower is still standing, but the second level has crumbled. In the track's heyday, the tower had provisions for people to stand on the roof, which provided an awesome view of the racing action. Unfortunately, that view is long gone. (Photo Courtesy www.waterwinterwonderland.com)

OSWEGO DRAGWAY

The landscape of the track was unique in that the racing surface was the highest point of the property, making an interesting view for the spectators. Here, a single-engine dragster is facing off against Norbert Locke's twin-flathead–powered dragster at Oswego. The worm's-eye view was great for photographers, as it provided a fantastic low-angle shot. (Photo Courtesy Norbert Locke)

Oswego, Illinois
1955–1979

Current Status: ➤ **ABANDONED**

Many of the tracks built during or before 1955 were simply repurposed runways on the site of abandoned airports. The surplus of military airfields after World War II made it easy for gearheads across the country to go fast in a straight line without fear of local law enforcement. Purpose-built drag strips were few and far between, but a once-quaint piece of farmland in Oswego, Illinois, will go down in history as one of the first purpose-built tracks in the United States.

Opening its doors in 1955, Oswego Dragway became a go-to hangout for the youth in the greater Chicago area, but increasingly fierce competition made it much more than a hangout for diehard racers.

The track got its start after Dale and Darold Cutsinger encouraged friends and fellow car guys Dan and Wally Smith to build a drag strip on their piece of property just outside Oswego on U.S. Route 34. The Smith brothers had inherited the farmland from their parents. Little motivation was needed to get started on the drag strip, but Oswego Dragway certainly didn't start out as a glamorous race facility. In fact, the first few gatherings involved drag racing on dirt, which was plenty of fun, but it was quickly decided that a paved racing surface would be a lot more consistent and offer higher speeds.

By 1956, Oswego Dragway was a fully paved quarter-mile drag strip, and the Smith brothers worked hard to manage the track. When it required upkeep, numerous car clubs

volunteered to help, including the Aurora Autocrats, the Traction Masters, and the Bearing Busters, just to name a few.

As evidenced by photographs of Oswego Dragway, the racing surface was the highest point of the property, making it great for water drainage, with an interesting view for spectators. Although no one had any real comparison in the early days, most drag strips' bleachers were positioned so that the audience looked down on the cars. Oswego's landscape offered somewhat of a worm's-eye view, but the lack of guardrails gave spectators a great view of the cars as the motored down the quarter-mile. Photographers didn't need to crouch down to get a cool shot of a car leaving the line, as the track's elevated surface did the hard work for them!

The track had great success and many racers remember certain person who was a staple at Oswego in the early days Jim "Woody" Woodrow. Oswego's flag starter, Woody had an unforgettable presence and lots of personality. His enthusiastic flag starts made him popular, but it was his white pants white shoes, and blue jacket that most folks remember the most. Characters like Woody burned long-lasting memories into the minds of children, teenagers, and young adults who visited the track, while also entertaining the regulars.

As Oswego continued to grow, the cars went faster and drag racing eventually outgrew its roots. The flag starter was replaced by automated lights and the timing system was updated as technology became available. Throughout the 1960s, the track catered to all sorts of drag racers, but Oswego made a name for itself in the 1970s as one of the nation's premier "doorslammer" tracks. With up-and-coming classes like Hot Rod and Pro Stock, which were very popular in the

This view shows the track's landscape even better, as a few youngsters watch a funny car leave the line. The banked shoulders of the track made for an interesting ride if you veered off course, but steel guardrails protected the spectators. (Photo Courtesy Brent Fregin)

Oswego provided plenty of wiggle room but don't be fooled by the expanse of grass between the track and the guardrail, because it is slightly banked. Oswego was the site of a major crash for Bill "Grumpy" Jenkins during a big match race in 1977, which left his Pro Stock Monza atop the guardrail. (Photo Courtesy Brent Fregin)

The unpaved pits weren't exactly luxurious, but that was part of the fun of racing at Oswego. You can see the simple timing tower on the left, with restrooms and concession stand on the right. Taken in 1970, this photo shows a diverse group of cars in the pits and parking area. (Photo Courtesy Brent Fregin)

"Animal Jim" Feurer, as he is affectionately known, launches hard in his wicked 1957 Mercury, which had a 427-ci Tunnel Port engine, backed by a four-speed manual transmission. Feurer was a regular at Oswego, taking home back-to-back track championships. This car was known for its wheels-up launches, and Animal Jim still owns it to this day. (Photo Courtesy Brent Fregin)

When Oswego Dragway closed in 1979, the track was stripped of its buildings and equipment, leaving only a strip of pavement on the property. The overgrowth was caused by a nursery, which used the property to grow trees for several years. The property has now been annexed into the city of Oswego and zoned as commercial. (Photo Courtesy Greg Rourke)

During a reconfiguration of the facility, the track actually swapped ends, which positioned its staging lanes and starting line very close to nearby streets. This proximity to the road, combined with the expanding neighborhoods in the area, ultimately led to the end of the Oswego era. (Photo Courtesy Greg Rourke)

The closing of Oswego Dragway was not well received by local racers, but after the change in ownership, there was little they could do about it. The property has been used by King Nursery for several years, but it may see some major changes, now that property zoning has changed. (Photo Courtesy Greg Rourke)

Midwest and the AHRA circuit, Oswego flourished with big-time events on a regular basis. While dragsters and funny cars still carried a huge wow factor for spectators, the doorslammers were just as exciting with high-RPM, wheels-up action.

One of the most memorable machines to race at Oswego was Jim Feurer's bright orange 1957 Mercury, aptly named *The Big Animal*. Weighing 4,000 pounds, the big sedan had a 427-ci Ford Tunnel Port engine, backed by a four-speed manual transmission. His first time at a serious race, Jim took home the victory in the 1D/Hot Rod class and was later Oswego's track champion in both 1973 and 1974. "Animal Jim," as he was known, then stepped up to the Pro Stock class and had great success with a wild Mercury Zephyr. While it's tough to single out one guy's car(s), it's also easy to see how Animal Jim became a household name, and a fan favorite at Oswego Dragway.

Eventually, the Oswego Dragway property was sold to Howard Koch, who closed the track for good in 1979 for unknown reasons. Some say that he bought the property with the intention of closing it, while others say that it closed because of the poor economy and lack of attendance. Either way, it was never again used as a drag strip. Instead, it became part of King Nursery, with trees overtaking both sides of the pavement, which remains intact for the most part. The trees take away from the track's elevated stance, and a lonely strip of pavement is all that's left of the old track.

Unfortunately, the property has been annexed into Oswego and zoned for commercial use. What little remains of Oswego Dragway provides a tiny glimpse into the past, but it's enough to bring back nearly twenty-five years of great memories of one of the first purpose-built drag strips in the country.

The entire length of the track's surface is still somewhat intact, from the burnout box to the shutdown area. More than thirty years of neglect has caused the asphalt racing surface to crack, and the overgrowth of the property certainly hasn't helped preserve the surface. Thousands of competition cars used this pavement from 1956 to the track's final event in 1979. Local veterinarian Howard Koch bought the property and closed the track shortly thereafter. (Photo Courtesy Greg Rourke)

U.S. 30 DRAG STRIP

U.S. 30 Drag Strip was home to lots of major Funny Car races, including the Coca-Cola Cavalcade of Stars events, created by track operator Ben Christ in 1969. Spectators also saw plenty of Funny Car action at many match races, as well as the AHRA national events held at U.S. 30. (Photo Courtesy Larry Rzepczynski)

Gary, Indiana
1957–1984

Current Status: ➤ **ABANDONED**

U.S. 30 Drag Strip, named for its close proximity to the highway of the same name, got its start in the late 1950s. Its location was perfect for racers in the greater Chicago area, while also catering to northern Indiana racers, as well as the southern Michigan crowd. U.S. 30 Drag Strip was built just south of Gary, Indiana, and ran alongside the famous Lincoln Highway, also known as U.S. Route 30. Another track with a nearly identical name resided in York,

Pennsylvania, but most folks referred to it as York U.S. 30 to reduce the confusion. Unfortunately, neither of the U.S. 30 tracks stood the test of time, but both enjoyed years of great success. The one in York is now an airport, and the one featured here sits abandoned in what is now Hobart, Indiana.

In its day, U.S. 30 Drag Strip was a top-of-the-line track and had a great run until its demise in 1984. This track started life as a project handled by a group of investors who sought

U.S. 30 Drag Strip was a popular destination for drag racers, especially those in the greater Chicago area. In the early days, the track featured a separate strip of pavement for each lane, with a strip of grass between them. This shot from the 1960s provides a nice view of the spectator seating arrangement and timing tower. (Photo Courtesy Larry Rzepczynski)

This shot of a jet-car match race shows the track after a few upgrades, including paving the strip of grass between th two lanes. Jet-car racing eventually caused major problems for the track, as the local government enforced a strict nois ordinance that required a special permit for any event featuring jet cars. (Photo Courtesy Larry Rzepczynski)

...he track was always considered a well-equipped facility that catered to its racers and spectators. Here, Chris "The ...reek" Karamesines is strapped into his fuel dragster, which is sitting atop the in-ground rollers. In the background is ...e new timing tower, which didn't see many years of use. (Photo Courtesy Mike Sopko)

...rn Moats is seen leaving the line at U.S. 30 during the track's last season. The 1984 AHRA Grand American Nationals ...as one of the last big meets for the northern Indiana track. Note the U.S. 30 AHRA shield logo painted between the ...nes. (Photo Courtesy Mike Sopko)

to take racing off the street and provide gearheads with a safe, legitimate place to race. It was constructed by the National Timing Association, under the supervision of the Northern Indiana Timing Association.

In an article in the September 21, 1957, issue of *Drag News* magazine, the drag strip received great praise, including an endorsement from N. Perry Luster, a drag racing insurance executive from the National Racing Affiliates. Luster said that U.S. 30 was the "best and safest drag strip" he has seen, just before its grand opening event on September 22, 1957. According to local racers, the track was actually open before that date, but the grand opening served as the big kickoff event to start regular weekly racing.

The track was built on 138 acres and featured 4,000 feet of pavement, which provided plenty of stopping room. Fosdick timing equipment was used to record the elapsed times and speeds for each racer, and there was even a reward for the first cars to break the 125- and 150-mph barriers. The track reportedly had a seating capacity of 5,000 in those early days, but that number was ultimately expanded when the track really hit its stride in the 1960s and 1970s. Early on, the track also featured two separate strips of asphalt, with a strip of grass separating them. This was later filled in across the main racing surface, but the shutdown area still had the twin strips of asphalt. Without question, it made for some wild rides.

Most folks who raced at U.S. 30 will tell you that the heyday of the track was during the Ben Christ era. Christ operated the track with great confidence, and promoted it in a manner that set the standard for drag strip owners, operators and managers across the country. Christ exercised his marketing skills to a high degree and the success of his tracks proved that it was worth the effort. Big events brought in thousands of spectators, which helped him make great profits at all of his tracks. He also operated Oswego Dragway for several years and had a hand in many other tracks' success.

Christ owned a drag strip management company called The Gold Agency, which helped a number of tracks promote races and attract spectators. This company also created the

Looking down track in this shot from 1992, you can see that the guardrails are still in place and the racing surface is in very poor condition, after just eight years of neglect. The signature grass in the center of the track's two lanes eventually overtook the pavement between them once again. (Photo Courtesy Mike Sopko)

n 1992, the tower still stood tall, and all of the track's bleachers and guardrails were still intact. At some point, the track vas stripped and the buildings were torn down, leaving only the pavement to tell the story. (Photo Courtesy Mike Sopko)

Veeds, grass, and trees gradually overtook the property as it sat vacant. It was annexed into the city of Hobart, Indiana, 1994, and remained on the market for more than a decade longer. It was eventually bought by a development com-any, but is still intact. (Photo Courtesy Mike Sopko)

Coca-Cola Cavalcade of Stars, which was a big-time promotional event featuring the very best funny cars and drivers in the sport. The Cavalcade events, which were held at several drag strips besides U.S. 30, featured a match-race-style atmosphere with a uniquely structured racing bracket, instead of the standard elimination bracket. The structure of these Coca-Cola-sponsored events catered heavily to spectators, allowing them to see lots of great action, so it was a huge success from its inception in 1969 to its final event in 1976.

During its most popular years, U.S. 30 Drag Strip was sanctioned by the AHRA, mainly because Christ had a large share in the sanctioning body for several of those years. The track was home to AHRA national events, as well as Christ's big promotional events and match races. He kept the U.S. 30 schedule packed with great action. He even scheduled big-name match races on Wednesday nights, giving folks a great excuse to go to the drag strip more than once a week.

All this success should've held some serious weight with the local government, but it didn't stop them from enforcing a noise ordinance, which was put in place because of complaints from nearby neighborhoods. The ordinance was geared toward jet cars, requiring a special permit to be purchased by the track prior to the event, and only allowed four jet-car events per year. During these four events, a strict curfew of 10:00 pm was enforced. Drag strips have certainly overcome tougher obstacles, but at the end of the 1984 racing season, the land owner did not renew the lease. This led many to believe that the local government had something to do with the owner's decision.

After the drag strip closed in 1984, it was left untouched for at least a decade, according to Mike Sopko, who visited the track in 1992. The tower, buildings, and track surface remained intact, but the lack of activity had taken its toll on the pavement. In 1994, the property was annexed into the city of Hobart, Indiana, and it eventually changed hands another decade later. The new owners are property developers, meaning that the remains of U.S. 30 Drag Strip may not last forever.

Although all of the buildings and track equipment are long gone, the pavement is still there, with a rapidly fading U.S. 30 AHRA logo painted between the lanes. Telephone poles block the entrance to keep unauthorized visitors from blasting down the decrepit track, while vast overgrowth takes away from the nostalgic appeal of the hallowed grounds. Although several efforts have been made to revive the track, it isn't likely to happen, based on the increasing number of houses surrounding the property. Eventually it will become yet another subdivision, but for now, it provides a glimpse into the glory days of Midwestern drag racing.

Current-day photos from U.S. 30 Drag Strip aren't nearly as exciting, as all of the buildings and track equipment are long gone. No more guardrails, no more light poles, and no more timing tower—all that's left is an expanse of pavement that saw more than twenty-five years of great racing action. (Photo Courtesy Mike Sopko)

CHAPTER 5

EAST-BOUND AND DOWN

As we continue eastward on our trek to find the coolest abandoned drag strips in the country, the terrain becomes a little rougher, and it's easy to see why it was more popular to build tracks out West. The hilly lands of Pennsylvania, and many of its neighboring states to the north, cost additional time and money to build a drag strip, but that didn't hinder the determined drag racing enthusiasts of the late 1950s.

By the end of the 1960s, a plethora of tracks had been built in numerous Northeastern states, most of which no longer exist. Fortunately, the hallowed grounds of many of these historic racing facilities remain, although dismantled with very few artifacts left behind.

The Northeast had many drag strips, but the extreme northern areas didn't have the drag racing fever, due to the inclement seasonal weather conditions. The weather, along

with the quickly developing eastern seaboard, meant that Northeastern drag strips had a hard time standing the test of time. Growing populations have been a big killer of all sorts of race tracks, so the influx in the late 1950s and early 1960s eventually led to the demise of several well-known drag strips.

At one time there were three tracks on Long Island alone, but none of them survived the growth of the area. And while many other tracks were in rural areas, a general lack of interest and a poor economy brought an end to several racing facilities. Other reasons, involving local governments and complaining neighbors, were among the causes of many track closings, which was a common problem across the country from the early 1970s to today.

Track landscapes and designs here were different than in any regions to the west, but they made for some very interesting

The Northeast had an excellent mix of drag cars, especially in the late 1960s when Super Stock began to evolve into more aggressive classes, such as Pro Stock. Car technology came a long way during the 1960s, even for stock-body doorslammers such as this *Locomotion* 1968 Camaro at Dover Drag Strip. Big power and better tires helped these cars get down the track. (Photo by T. O'Shea, Courtesy www.doverdragstrip.com)

Drag racing was huge in the Northeast, but the farther north you went, the less active the drag strips were due to the long, harsh winters. A variety of drag strips had wintertime drags, but the majority of racing took place from April to October. (Photo by T. O'Shea, Courtesy www.doverdragstrip.com)

facilities. Many were built by scooping out enough earth for a flat racing surface, leaving the shutdown area and spectator areas rather hilly. This was also common practice in the South, as the mountainous terrain made it difficult to completely restructure an entire piece of property, where track owners could easily dig just enough for the track itself.

This variety in landscape made for a different spectator experience from track to track, as the seating arrangements were generally based on the lay of the land. Some tracks positioned the spectators on the main level, while others had the spectators looking down on the cars. Either way, Northeastern tracks had plenty of character, which make them fairly easy to identify from photographs.

As for the cars that made Northeastern drag racing so popular, doorslammers played a big role, whether they ran in the Gas classes, Altered classes, or Stock classes. With easy access to chassis builders and "store bought" dragster frames, it was no wonder the West Coast racing crowd had a heavy dragster influence in the late 1950s. Companies such as Chassis Research and Dragmaster supplied ready-to-run chassis setups, but they catered mainly to West Coast racers.

In this region of the United States, many of the areas were a bit hilly, so some tracks had to be carved out of the hills. Some areas, such as Long Island, New York (which had three drag strips in the 1960s), took advantage of the land near water, as it was much flatter. (Photo by T. O'Shea, Courtesy www.doverdragstrip.com)

The long shipping distance and high cost led many East Coast racers to build their own dragsters, until Pat Bilbow started selling altered roadster and dragster chassis in 1959. He built the frames in his shop, Lyndwood Welding. His work helped shape the drag racing scene in the Northeast by providing racers with quality frames that normally weren't accessible. From 1959 to 1964, Pat built a few hundred dragster frames under the Lyndwood name, meaning that there was a Lyndwood chassis–equipped rail racing at most Northern tracks pretty much every weekend. These days, Pat's son Bob Bilbow campaigns his father's personal dragster, which has been immaculately restored to its early-1960s configuration.

Regardless of the Eastern dragster deficiency, the drag racing scene was as hot as in any other part of the country. Pennsylvania had several drag strips on both sides of the state, while Maryland had a few tracks of its own. Big-name tracks such as New York National Speedway, Pittsburgh International Dragway, and Connecticut Dragway drew enormous crowds on a regular basis, while the smaller tracks enjoye success as well.

Unfortunately, many of the tracks did not survive th wrath of the general public and its hatred for all things loud fast, and dangerous. It ultimately hurt the sport of drag rac ing, but the hardcore guys still found a place to race, even if meant they had to make a long haul to the track. This enthus asm has kept the sport alive, but the future of this drag racin lifestyle shouldn't be taken for granted.

New laws and regulations can bring a track's success to screeching halt, which means that historic track owners hav to hope for the best and continue to uphold their respectiv legacies. Dedicated gearheads with an undeniable passion fo drag racing have kept this sport afloat, and you can bet they' fight for their right to race, regardless of their location. Th Northeast was made up of wild cars, unforgettable driver and unique drag strips, which resulted in a combination tha left many young car enthusiasts hooked for life.

Pat Bilbow made a big impact on the regional drag racing scene by developing a "store bought" dragster chassis, built in his shop, Lyndwood Welding, in Wilkes-Barre, Pennsylvania. These new dragster frames, known as the Eliminator, were a huge hit in the Northeast, giving racers an alternative to the homemade dragsters of the era. (Photo by Dick Donofrio, Courtesy www.doverdragstrip.com)

DOVER DRAG STRIP

The front gate had a ticket booth with a very short list of demands: Pay $2 for general admission and don't bring alcohol into the facility. Other than that, the rules were fairly relaxed, which always makes for a good time. (Photo by T. O'Shea, Courtesy www.doverdragstrip.com)

Wingdale, New York
1961-1976

Current Status: ➤ **ABANDONED**

The birth of East Coast drag racing was a few years after the big boom in California, and it even came after the Midwest car guys formed a few race tracks atop their farm land. The late 1950s saw an increase in East Coast hot rod activity, so folks scrambled to find places to race, without the risk of getting caught by local law enforcement. From small towns to bigger cities, the drag racing scene in the Northeast was on the rise. In New York state, drag racing got its start in 1959, when racers assembled in Montgomery to race at the airport. Quarter-mile races were held with times and speeds recorded with less-than-optimal equipment. Being the first of its type in the area, drag racing was very popular and drew crowds from surrounding towns, counties, and states.

One particular weekend, Mark Mastriani and the Danbury Modifiers traveled to Montgomery for a race. Chet Anderson from Brookfield, Connecticut, rode with Mastriani in his 1955 Chevy to see what drag racing was all about. While Mastriani raced his car, Anderson spent a great deal of time checking out the surroundings. The very next day, Anderson began searching for a place to build his own track in Connecticut. He had met Frank Marrata at Montgomery and asked him to be his partner.

Marrata ultimately turned him down on the business offer, but later built Connecticut Dragway in East Haddem, Connecticut. Regardless of his failed attempt at a partnership, Anderson purchased 144 acres of farmland in Wingdale, New

Thousands of drag racers saw this sign at one point or another during Dover Drag Strip's existence. The custom lettering and dragster character gave the sign a distinct look that was easily identifiable. The small town of Wingdale, New York, was the home of Dover Drag Strip. (Photo by T. O'Shea, Courtesy www.doverdragstrip.com)

Track photographer T. O'Shea did a magnificent job of documenting the history of Dover Drag Strip with thousands of photos during the track's operation. The timing tower was placed on the pit side (right lane) of the track, and acted as a great backdrop for photos. This is a great shot of the tower in the track's heyday. (Photo by T. O'Shea, Courtesy www.doverdragstrip.com)

Dover's wide lanes offered plenty of room to reel in a squirrely race car. The track had lots of character, but that didn't equate to very high safety standards. The track managed to land an NHRA sanction, but it only lasted a short while due to the track's lack of safety equipment, such as guardrails. (Photo by T. O'Shea, Courtesy www.doverdragstrip.com)

York. After acquiring the property, Joe Archiere entered the picture as a business partner, who just so happened to have the heavy equipment to build the track.

Anderson and Archiere opened the track on May 14, 1961, and called it Dover Drag Strip. They enlisted the help of the Danbury Modifiers car club to be the crew and inspectors. Before any of the track workers arrived that morning, a 1959 Pontiac was already parked at the gate in anticipation of the first race. In fact, the determined gearhead had spent the night in his car to make sure he was first in line at the new drag strip. The man in the Pontiac was James "Grover" Grove, who became the first paid customer and still has the ticket.

As the track grew in popularity, it needed some form of guidance, so Charles "Van" Van Muren was hired as the Dover's first track manager. Before the Christmas tree was installed, the track's flagman starter was George Hosford, who was known for his acrobatics. Al Svarplaitis also served as starter. In terms of management, Tim Hallock took over in 1962 followed by several others. Joe Tanner held the longest term as manager, as he ran the track from 1965 until 1973. Chris Swift was the track's final manager, staying until the final race in 1976.

Track announcers were Harry "Blue Goose" Loper, followed by Ralph "Chink" Butera, Gary Teto, and then Dino "Weirdo" Lawrence from 1965 to 1972. Joe Tanner's son Charlie took over until Dover closed its doors. Frank Rice and Mike Mannion ran and repaired the timing clocks. Other details include the concession stand, which was always run by the American Legion.

Though it was only sanctioned by the NHRA for one year, the track enjoyed lots of success, but it did have its share

The action at Dover Drag Strip was always worth the price of admission. Big-time match races were common, but the regular racing program offered plenty of excitement. In this photo, Gary Balfe's *Trap Tripper* 1957 Chevy station wagon does battle against a hard-launching, big-block Corvette. (Photo by T. O'Shea, Courtesy www. doverdragstrip.com)

This shot provides an excellent view of the racing surface, as a dragster begins to haze the tires off the line. The tower is in clear view, and you can also see the spectators lined up atop the banked sidelines of the drag strip. (Photo by T. O'Shea, Courtesy www.doverdragstrip.com)

When the big names came to town Dover Drag Strip filled up with spectators. One such instance was when Bill Shrewsberry's *L.A. Dart* made its way to Dover. The rear-engine Dart toured the country doing wheelstands for as long as the track allowed. Here, even the rear wheels are airborne, while a huge crowd watches in amazement. (Photo by T. O'Shea, Courtesy www.doverdragstrip.com)

of safety concerns, which may be the reason behind NHRA pulling out. A harsh dropoff on the left side of the shutdown area, and less-than-adequate guardrails probably didn't pass NHRA's regulations, so it was a short-lived sanction from the well-known organization.

The 1970s was a tough time for drag strips across the country, and Dover was no exception. It suffered from low attendance, which was due to small payouts and a severe lack of updates to the facility. Dover went its entire course of operation without finish-line scoreboards, and while other tracks eventually updated their equipment, Dover stuck with what it had. Also remember that the 1970s was a tough time for all gearheads because of high gas prices and strict emission standards. It was simply a slump that Dover couldn't overcome, especially when you consider the offer that Anderson and Archiere got for the property.

After the track closed its doors on May 23, 1976, the property was used to harvest peat moss. During the digging workers hit a natural spring, which created a sizable lake, just a few feet from what remained of the track's shutdown area.

Today, the track's original landscape has changed drastically. Most of the track's surface is long gone, aside from the shutdown area, but lots of memories reside in this historic New York drag strip. Sure, there were plenty of other tracks in New York, including several popular destinations on Long Island, but Dover Drag Strip held a special place in hundreds of racers' hearts, and still does to this day. In fact, Ron Frost, a longtime Dover attendee and racer, requested to have his ashes spread on the track's property when he passed away. His time came a few years ago and his request was granted, with the funeral held in the shutdown area of Dover.

Unfortunately, when the track closed in 1976, the property did not stand the test of time. Miners harvesting peat moss happened to strike a natural spring in the process. This created a large lake very close to the old racing surface. The other areas were abandoned. (Photo by Tink Shaefer, Courtesy www.doverdragstrip.com)

When the new property owners stripped the track of all drag racing equipment, they did very little to retain the old pavement used for the racing surface. These days it is mostly overgrown, with only a few areas of the shutdown area showing through the weeds. (Photo by Tink Shaefer, Courtesy www.doverdragstrip.com)

It's a shame that the distinct landscape of Dover Drag Strip has been completely removed with the intense mining. The track had lots of local history, but almost all of it is gone, aside from this wide patch of pavement in what used to be the shutdown area. (Photo Courtesy John Shiner)

This shot offers an incredible view of the drag racing scene at PID, with stock-bodied racers in the downhill staging lanes. Just beyond the cars in the foreground are a couple of motorcycles launching off the line. The deep valley had to be tricky in the drag strip's previous life as an airport. (Photo Courtesy Bill Truby)

Bridgeville, Pennsylvania
1964–1976

Current Status: ➤ **ABANDONED**

There's no doubt that the Northeast had its share of great drag strips, but the western Pennsylvania guys cannot deny the impact Pittsburgh International Dragway (PID) had on the local racing scene. With a location just southwest of Pittsburgh, the track had a great following, and has an interesting history.

PID started its life as Campbell Airport, which was located in a hollow and built by Charles E. Campbell in the late 1950s. The airport had a unique landscape, as it rested in a deep valley and shared an entrance with the Charles E. Camp-

bell Coal Company's Maude Mine. The mine operated from 1949 to 1962, and the Campbell Airport's first location was in operation until 1962, which was a turning point in Campbell's businesses. The valley configuration didn't provide great conditions for flying, so he moved the airport to the top of the hill, leaving the old runway unused.

Since PID started life as an airport, it had plenty of length for a quarter-mile track, and the mining operation meant that heavy-duty scales were already on the property. This meant Campbell had to put out very little effort to initially open the

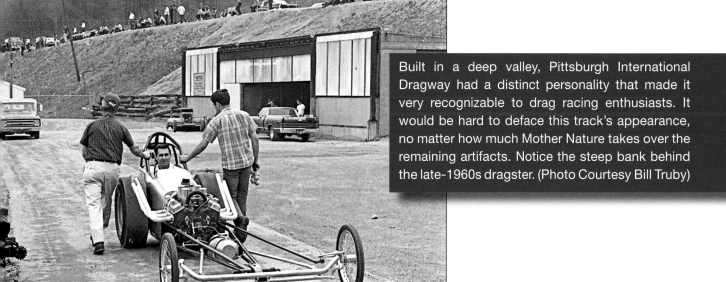

Built in a deep valley, Pittsburgh International Dragway had a distinct personality that made it very recognizable to drag racing enthusiasts. It would be hard to deface this track's appearance, no matter how much Mother Nature takes over the remaining artifacts. Notice the steep bank behind the late-1960s dragster. (Photo Courtesy Bill Truby)

rack and begin having races. That simplicity didn't last long or the unique Pennsylvania track drag as racing became more and more competitive with new rules and class designations.

The new racing facility became known as Pittsburgh International Dragway, and it quickly gained popularity as drag racing exploded into the car guy world in the early 1960s. Campbell partnered with Eddie Witzberger, who owned a nearby circle track, Heidelberg Raceway. Heidelberg was the home of NASCAR legend Lee Petty's first win, and was a popular track for many years.

Witzberger got into the drag racing industry after a local promoter encouraged him to hold drag races on the straightaway of Heidelberg Raceway, long before PID came on the scene. The local promoter who encouraged Witzberger to get

The Northeast had some wild creations in the 1960s, including this Henry J. Running in B/Altered, this car has an extreme amount of engine setback, as you can see by the injector stacks sitting where the driver normally resides. This angle also shows the steep banks and extreme landscape of PID. (Photo Courtesy Bill Truby)

Looking down the track as two gassers leave the line, you can see that PID actually had guardrails, which was rare during the 1960s. Notice also the uphill shutdown area, which was one reason people loved PID. An uphill shutdown area meant that you could usually coast back to the pits. (Photo Courtesy Bill Truby)

As time went on, the track grew in popularity and changed with the times. The retaining wall on the left side of the track wore huge "Pittsburgh International Dragway" signage, which always stood out in photos like this early 1970s matchup featuring an injected Hemi dragster and *The Fokky Farmer,* a Pinto funny car. (Photo Courtesy Bill Truby)

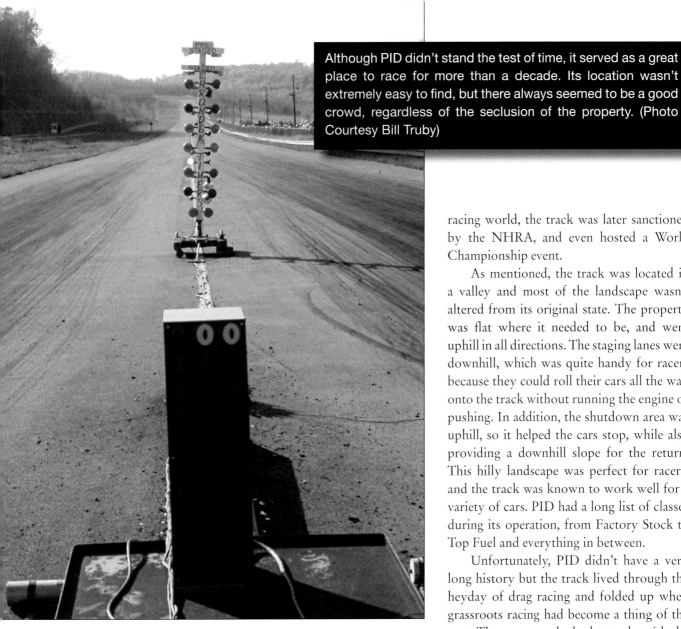

racing world, the track was later sanctioned by the NHRA, and even hosted a World Championship event.

As mentioned, the track was located in a valley and most of the landscape wasn't altered from its original state. The property was flat where it needed to be, and went uphill in all directions. The staging lanes were downhill, which was quite handy for racers because they could roll their cars all the way onto the track without running the engine or pushing. In addition, the shutdown area was uphill, so it helped the cars stop, while also providing a downhill slope for the return. This hilly landscape was perfect for racers, and the track was known to work well for a variety of cars. PID had a long list of classes during its operation, from Factory Stock to Top Fuel and everything in between.

Unfortunately, PID didn't have a very long history but the track lived through the heyday of drag racing and folded up when grassroots racing had become a thing of the past. The economy had a lot to do with the closure of PID but it was also related to a new drag strip that opened in the Pittsburgh area, Keystone Raceway Park. The new track's builder was none other than Walt Mentzer, one of the guys who helped manage PID in the early days. Keystone drew larger crowds, and is still in operation, although it has been renamed Pittsburgh Raceway Park after a change in ownership.

Due to a number of causes, PID closed its doors forever in 1976, leaving behind a legacy that many racers remember. The pavement is still there but badly damaged from years of neglect. Nothing else remains of the track but diehard PID supporters, including photographer Bill Truby, began holding a reunion event in 1997 at Pittsburgh Raceway Park, and still holds it every year. It allows the old racers, fans, and workers to relive the days of PID, even though the original track is nothing more than an overgrown strip of pavement today.

nto drag racing was Walt Mentzer, a Pittsburgh hot rodder who worked for the NHRA in the early 1950s, formed the NHRA in the mid 1950s, and helped form the NASCAR drag racing division in the 1960s. With an excellent resume, Mentzer was the perfect candidate to help build the drag strip and make it a great place to race.

The unique partnership meant that Campbell owned half of the circle track, and Witzberger owned half of the drag strip. Witzberger's involvement with NASCAR, along with Mentzer's willingness to work hard, helped create the NASCAR drag racing division, so PID was one of the first tracks to carry the sanction.

The NASCAR drag racing circuit had a great following of racers, which always influences spectator attendance. With big races on a regular basis, the track gained notoriety and quickly became a destination for the big names of the sport, be it for national events or match races. After NASCAR left the drag

The hilly property offered features that many drag strips lacked. Downhill staging lanes meant that you could coast to the strip as you waited your turn in line. The hills also helped the shutdown area, and gave the spectators an interesting view of the track while keeping them a safe distance from the action. (Photo Courtesy Bill Truby)

Although weeds and trees have taken over most of the property, the historic strip of pavement is still there and the general lay of the land is the same. (Photo Courtesy Bill Truby)

A narrow strip of the pavement has resisted the overgrowth of weeds and trees, but the property has the potential to be cleaned up in order to preserve the old pavement. PID reunion events are currently held at Pittsburgh Raceway Park, which was once a competing track in the area. (Photo Courtesy Bill Truby)

Big cracks and missing chunks of pavement indicate that PID has seen better days. It had a very good surface in its heyday, but the cracks are a reminder that Mother Nature has not been kind to this legendary Pennsylvania drag strip. (Photo Courtesy Bill Truby)

Part of a building still stands on the property, but just barely due to the years of abandonment. Although the property is in sad shape, this wide clearing offers another good view of the valley, which had an echoing roar that lasted from 1964 to 1976. (Photo Courtesy Bill Truby)

CONNECTICUT DRAGWAY

Connecticut Dragway gave hot rodders and racers in the more extreme Northeastern areas a great place to race. This shot of the pits and staging lanes shows a great selection of cars at one of its many Funny Car meets in the early 1970s. (Photo Courtesy Bob Snyder)

East Haddam, Connecticut
1961-1985

Current Status: ➤ **TEST TRACK FOR *CONSUMER REPORTS***

In the Northeast, the farther north you go, the fewer drag strips you find. The harsh winters and short summers are simply not conducive to drag racing. In Connecticut, there was only one drag strip, Connecticut Dragway.

Located in the small town of East Haddam, most folks considered Connecticut Dragway to be located in Colchester, as the old highway maps rarely listed East Haddam. Unlike today when we rely so heavily on our phones and GPS devices to get us where we're going, old-time racers knew that if you found Colchester you were close enough to ask for directions, or at least follow another racer to the track. Connecticut Dragway quickly became a hotspot for North-

eastern racers and drew big crowds because of its action packed event schedule.

The track got its start in 1961, when Frank Marratta built it from the ground up as a purpose-built drag strip. Most tracks from the late 1950s and early 1960s were originally airport runways, but Connecticut Dragway was built specifically for racing. Marratta had been exposed to drag racing years prior, and actually received an offer to become a partner in the Dover Drag Strip project less than a year before opening his own track. Without question, going out on his own was a gamble, but it paid off as the track saw lots of success through the years.

During the 1960s, Connecticut Dragway had numerous big-name match races and other major events. It carried that momentum into the late 1960s and early 1970s when funny cars reigned supreme. Huge funny car events made the track famous, and the wide-open feel of the track inspired quite a bit of confidence in the drivers of the era. With no guardrails lining the pavement, racers had a bit of space to reel in their race cars before actually making contact with anything. It certainly made for exciting racing, especially when all the big dogs rolled into town.

The track continued to prosper, but felt the same effects of the economy as did many other drag strips in the United States. With little warning, the muscle car era ended and the general public suddenly became more interested in economy cars to fight the higher gas prices and insurance premiums. This sent a ripple through the industry, and by 1978, Connecticut Dragway closed its gates.

Fortunately, Marratta held on to the property and a group of racers and investors approached him about reopening the track. They were successful in bringing it back, and even renewed the NHRA sanction, but it was a short-lived success. Connecticut International Raceway, as it was known at the time, closed again at the end of the 1985 racing season.

The property remained untouched for many years until Consumers Union purchased the land several years ago. The company had previously rented racing facilities such as Lime

Connecticut Dragway had its share of wild action, especially in the heyday of funny car racing. This photo of two seemingly out-of-control funny cars—The *Illusion* in the far lane and Paul Stefansky's *Super 'Stang* in the near lane—is a great example of the crazy passes made by fearless drivers. The Christmas tree was very vulnerable, with absolutely no protection from Funny Car madness. (Photo Courtesy Bob Snyder)

The seldom-seen candy apple red *Jungle Jim* Camaro appeared at Connecticut Dragway in September 1970 at a huge Funny Car meet. This incredible shot of Jim Liberman battling Joe Petruccelli's *Super Twister* Camaro includes the unique, checkered boxes, which were a recognizable trait of the track. (Photo Courtesy Bob Snyder)

Speaking of that vulnerable Christmas tree, John Rodriques is in the process of plowing over it in his *Light My Fire* Corvette funny car. This car was well known in New England, and offered a level of excitement that always drew a crowd. This shot please provides a clear view of the timing tower, which still stands. (Photo Courtesy Bob Snyder)

Looking down track, you can see a very short stretch of guardrailing to protect the spectators, while the rest of the track had little in the way of barriers. The slightly banked grass shoulder really didn't help cars get straightened out, but the spectators were at a safe distance from the track. (Photo Courtesy Bob Snyder)

Wheelstanders were a popular exhibition vehicle in the heyday of drag racing, and they still get lots of attention these days. There was an abundance of wheelie machines in the 1970s, with plenty of alternative designs, such as the *Trash Truck*, a Chevy Corvair pickup. (Photo Courtesy Bob Snyder)

One of the best stories from Connecticut Dragway has to be the highly publicized match race between Frank Marratta, owner of the track, and Indy car legend Mario Andretti in 1968. The craziest part is the fact that it was scheduled for the Sunday of the Indy 500, which is generally a busy day for Indy racers. However, rain had pushed time trials onto Sunday's schedule, delaying the main event.

Andretti had qualified third for the 500, but flew in a private plane for the special match race in Connecticut. The plane landed on the drag strip(!) and Andretti hopped in a Tasca-prepped Cobra Jet Mustang to do battle with Marratta, who piloted a Norwood-prepped Camaro.

Both cars ran mid-11-second ETs, and Andretti didn't cut the track owner any slack. In fact, he won every round of the match race, and then flew back to Indianapolis, where he finished in the last position of the Indy 500, after only completing two laps when his engine blew.

Rock Park to keep all of their work and research in a consistent environment. The company owns *Consumer Reports*, which does a wide range of testing for various products, including new cars, trucks, and SUVs. The drag strip was resurfaced and reconfigured to include a driving course as well as two skid pads. *Consumer Reports* uses the 4,100-foot expanse of pavement for all sorts of testing, and puts all 327 acres of the property to use with intense off-road courses and many other test courses.

Although Connecticut Dragway will never again be used for its original purpose, it still lives on in the little town of East Haddam. The timing tower still stands on the property, which is considered a historical site. Unfortunately, Consumers Union does not open the facility to the public, and it is not accessible for viewing.

For the folks wanting to learn more about Connecticut Dragway or possibly see some of the awesome machinery that raced there many years ago, a reunion event is held every year, organized by the Connecticut Street Rod Association. As for the track, it will continue to see use by its new owners, which is a fate better than most tracks featured in this book.

The view of Connecticut Dragway is quite different these days, but the long, wide strip of pavement shares the same general characteristics. From the passenger seat of a 1955 Chevy gasser, you can get a feel for the nostalgic flavor, but modern buildings owned by Consumers Union disrupt the vintage track. (Photo Courtesy Trent Sherrill)

A long expanse of asphalt is mighty tempting when you have two nostalgic vehicles lined up. The new owners are not welcoming to many visitors, but the right connections got these two ex-racers into the facility for a photo shoot. The vastly renovated property now features a number of test tracks for modern vehicles. (Photo Courtesy Trent Sherrill)

Although it has been updated with a second-story deck and vinyl siding on the exterior, the timing tower still stands at the site of Connecticut Dragway. Signs that read "Historical District" are placed in front of the tower, which is an indication that Consumers Union takes the historic property seriously. (Photo Courtesy Trent Sherrill)

POCONO DRAG LODGE

Although it is difficult to make out the details in this mid-1960s photograph, an altered roadster is lining up on the star[t]ing line at Pocono Drag Lodge. Safety equipment is limited, as the only barrier between fans and the race track was [a] chain-link fence. Even the fence looks a bit unstable. (Photo Courtesy Jack Thomas)

Bear Creek, Pennsylvania
1963–1972

Current Status: ➤ **USED FO[R] POCONO REUNION EVENTS**

These days, if you enjoy going to the drag strip, you might daydream about what it would be like to have your own track. You might even drive by a piece of property and think, "That would make a great drag strip." Today, it would be completely absurd to come home from a local drag strip and decide to build your own. During the 1960s, however, it was a different ballgame and gearheads were not afraid to take a chance when it came to having another place to race. John Perugino and his sons Jim and Joe took that gamble and built Pocono Drag Lodge in 1963.

Perugino's inspiration for the drag strip was the Forty Fort Airport drags in Forty Fort, Pennsylvania. During the late 1950s, the airport held big drag racing events, and Perugino decided that a purpose-built drag strip would be a great opportunity for racers and spectators. So he and his two sons bought a piece of property in Bear Creek, Pennsylvania, and

broke ground on what became known as the Pocono Dra[g] Lodge (PDL).

PDL was home to lots of big-time racers, and the Perug[i]nos had huge plans for the facility; the drag strip was only o[ne] part. They planned to have other race tracks on the propert[y] as well as hotels in the surrounding area, but the rural loca[a]tion didn't lend itself well to the big plans. However, the trac[k] enjoyed lots of success in the heyday of drag racing, althoug[h] it didn't exactly explode onto the scene when it opened in th[e] summer of 1963. Even with the modest start, Pocono took o[ff] and found its niche, which gave the Peruginos peace of min[d] regarding their $360,000 investment. PDL was home to Supe[r] Stock races, as well as a number of dragster-based event[s] which were popular in the 1960s all across the United States[.]

During the track's operation, it had a number of A-li[st] drag racers blast down its quarter mile of asphalt. PDL w[as]

Here, Tim Richard's 1963 Plymouth pulls up to staging at Pocono Drag Lodge. The Northeast had a great Super Stock following, and it made for some awesome door-to-door drag racing. Funny cars eventually took the limelight, but super stockers stayed relevant for quite some time. (Photo Courtesy Jack Thomas)

the home track for five-time NHRA champion Joe Amato long before he made the big time with his Top Fuel dragster efforts. The track was never home to any groundbreaking events in the NHRA or AHRA world, but it certainly provided a great place to race for many racers, especially those in northeast Pennsylvania. Like most tracks, PDL had many high-level match races, which consistently drew big crowds and kept the track on everyone's radar.

The track's luck ran out in the summer of 1972, when Hurricane Agnes tore through the Northeast. The hurricane left behind a devastating trail of damage from the overwhelming floods. The drag strip didn't receive much damage, but Perugino's construction business took his focus during the rebuilding of the surrounding communities. During this time, drag strip operations were postponed, but it wasn't made known that the track would not reopen until later in the year. The hurricane hit at about the same time as the end of the muscle car era, which caused a severe downward spiral in the car guy world. This lack of interest led the Perugino family to officially close PDL and focus on the construction business.

Fast forward nearly forty years, the track remained vacant until Charlie Hulsizer took the initiative to create a PDL reunion. The idea involved cleaning up the abandoned property and holding a car show on the actual drag strip. Obviously, this required permission from the owners, which happened to be Joe Perugino, who was very receptive to the event idea. Hulsizer had never actually attended PDL during its operation, but his desire to bring back those memories resulted in many hours of work to prepare the property for an event of this magnitude.

Hulsizer found that the property still had many of the landmarks that had made the track special. He found engine parts and other artifacts, proving that the Peruginos literally walked away from the property and never even had the desire to clear it out. Luckily, the property stayed in the family and didn't fall victim to further development.

A crewman preps the track for Al Graeber's burnout in his wild Dodge Charger funny car named *Tickle Me Pink*. Although the black-and-white picture doesn't do the paint job much justice, the pink funny car was hard to miss! This shot provides a view of the right side of the track—mostly open, with bleachers farther to the right. (Photo Courtesy Jack Thomas)

Like many other tracks, Pocono Drag Lodge had its share of high-stakes match races and Funny Car events. Here, "Jungle" Jim Liberman debuts his newest funny car—it's so new that the body was still in primer. This photo also provides a good look at the tower. (Photo Courtesy Jack Thomas)

George Whalen campaigne this awesome Barracuda funn car and was a regular at man Northeastern tracks, incluc ing PDL. This shot has anothe great view of the timing towe as well as the lack of guarc rails, with spectators sitting o the embankment, no more tha 10 feet from the racing surface (Photo Courtesy Jack Thomas

This photo of the poorly preserved track was taken in 1989. The tower, although beaten by the harsh winters, still stood, wearing its signature lettering. The years of neglect had taken a toll on all of the wooden structures on the property. (Photo Courtesy Stan Zigmont)

he ticket booth was also in sad shape in 989. Many of the artifacts from the track still emain, making it a great place for a reunion vent to relive the good ol' days of PDL. Folks ke Jack Thomas and Charlie Hulsizer have orked wonders on what's left of the historic ack. (Photo Courtesy Stan Zigmont)

In 1989, the wooden bleachers were badly worn. Considering that this picture was taken more than twenty years ago, the track is actually in better shape in its current condition, thanks to devoted fans. (Photo Courtesy Stan Zigmont)

ast forward to 2010 and those wooden bleachers are still on the PDL property, but they've suffered through another venty years of harsh weather. The bleachers are obviously not in use for the reunion events, but still rest on the property s an authentic artifact. (Photo Courtesy Stan Zigmont)

For the reunion events, signage has been recreated to look just like the old days at PDL. From the hand-painted sign in the foreground, to the white cone and signs between the lanes, this setup brings back lots of memories for Northeastern racers who cut their teeth at PDL. (Photo Courtesy Stan Zigmont)

Even though the track was in very poor shape when Hulsizer first saw it, he and many others worked hard to get it ready for the reunion. His efforts were successful, as the event went off without a hitch. It is now an annual show, where nostalgia drag cars can be seen, and all the old-time racers can swap stories about their time at PDL. It's generally held in the summer, and it's quickly growing into a must-attend event for anyone interested in the history of drag racing. Hulsizer and other PDL enthusiasts, including Jack Thomas, have recreated the magic of PDL by repainting the old tower to its former appearance. Unfortunately, a windstorm in early 2012 sent the tower toppling down, but a new structure is being built in its place to replicate the look of the original tower.

Other remaining features of PDL include the "Start" wording painted on the starting line and the "Finish" wording down track. The wooden bleachers are still around and the entire track surface is still there. In the shutdown area, the surrounding land was used for shale mining during the later years of the track's operation, which can be seen in some of the later photographs. After nearly forty years of growth, the earth had almost reclaimed the historic track, but thanks to countless hours of work, the Pocono Drag Lodge is back in action for one event per year: the Reunion.

Although weather had taken most of the structural stability from the original timing tower, the organizers of the reunion took the time to repair it and paint it to resemble the original. A windstorm blew this patched tower down, so a new one is in the works. (Photo Courtesy Stan Zigmont)

SOUTHERN COMFORT

Of the four major regions showcased in this book, the South is arguably packed with the most creative minds in the drag racing world. Granted, being creative doesn't always equal success, but it makes for an interesting experience—the Southern folks always put on a great show. This ingenuity was evident in the cars that raced in the South, as well as the tracks they raced on, thanks to the mountainous landscape in most areas. Simple solutions were created to overcome landscape issues, and if you had a bulldozer and access to an asphalt company, you could be in the business of drag racing. Fancy towers, high-tech timing equipment, and up-to-date safety features weren't on the radar for Southern track owners and racers quite yet, so the homegrown atmosphere was in full effect.

Although lots of small tracks gave Southerners plenty of places to race, many larger tracks were scattered in more populated areas, such as Dallas, Memphis, Atlanta, and other big cities. The larger tracks held national events for one of the big-three sanctioning bodies (NHRA, AHRA, or IHRA) while the smaller tracks held weekly racing events that kept racer and spectators intrigued. Obviously, the big events paid mor to win, but you can bet those small events drew a consister crowd in the heyday of the sport.

However, the South wasn't immune to the harsh econom that hit the rest of the country in the late 1970s. That econ omy caused a general lack of interest in drag racing, whic caused a ripple effect in the industry. The difference betwee the South and some of the other regions is that heightene safety precautions and insurance regulations had already pu an end to many drag strips before the poor economy coul cause a problem.

The South was once known for its outlaw tracks and th exciting racing it produced. The tracks had minimal safet equipment and a "no rules" attitude for spectators, so the lev of danger was part of the fun. Brave spectators watched th racing action from a very close vantage point and the racer dealt with poor track conditions on a regular basis—two con ditions that do not mix well.

Drag racing in the South had a huge element of danger, not only for the racers but also for the spectators. As you ca see in this picture from Paradise Drag Strip in Calhoun, Georgia, spectators lined the wooden guardrails, and eve propped up their feet on the rail as Howard Neal and Robert Nance leave the line. (Photo Courtesy Walter Parsons)

ichard Petty's infamous Barracuda drag car is seen here at the AHRA Winternationals held at Bee Line Dragway in late anuary 1965. This was the first event that featured a class for cars that pushed the limits of Super Stock. The new Super tock Experimental evolved into what we now call Funny Cars. (Photo Courtesy John Durand)

After Petty's unfortunate accident at Southeastern International Dragway in February 1965, he had mixed emotions about getting back into the drag racing world. He quickly rebounded and built this car to fulfill prior match race commitments, after burying the *Outlawed* car behind his shop. Petty's drag racing career ended when NASCAR lifted the Hemi ban later in 1965. (Photo Courtesy Blue Ridge Institute & Museum of Ferrum College)

The turning point for Southern tracks came in the late 960s, as the cars began outgrowing the race tracks, which d to numerous crashes and injuries. The growing number f crashes and the accompanying rules and regulations caused any tracks to close their gates forever.

The First of Several

Drag racing has an exceptional record when it comes to pectator safety, which is especially remarkable considering he wild nature of racing in the 1950s and 1960s. Class evolu- on and innovation made for unpredictable moments, so the kelihood of tragic accidents was rather high. One of the first ccidents that sparked some debate on the safety of drag strips nd race cars occurred at Southeastern International Drag- ay, a quarter-mile drag strip in Dallas, Georgia, just outside tlanta. The track was a great facility at the time, but nothing ould prepare it for a freak accident.

Part of what makes this example so memorable is the acer involved. It was none other than NASCAR legend ichard Petty. He's always been known for his blue number

43 round-track vehicles, but he did try his hand at drag racing for a short time.

The reason for his dabbling in drag racing is quite simple. When NASCAR banned the Hemi (and the Ford overhead cam engine) at the end of the 1964 season, Petty decided to boycott the series. Some Mopar racers moved to the USAC racing series, but Petty chose drag racing to fill his racing void and support the folks at Mopar for building such an incredible engine. He and his crew built a 1964 Plymouth Barracuda, and fit it with a 426-ci Hemi engine. The car wore the fitting name of *Outlawed* and even had lettering on the back that said, "NASCAR: If you can't outrun 'em, outlaw 'em."

Richard Petty's Barracuda wasn't built to fit a particular class such as Super Stock. It was mainly used for match races, which garnered way more attention, and offered much more excitement for the spectators. He wasted little time getting the Barracuda on the ground; February 28, 1965, proved to be a tough day for "The King."

Petty had organized a best-of-three match race with Arnie Beswick, another icon of the era. During one of the passes,

Petty's car broke a component in the suspension, sending it off course. With no chance of saving it, Petty tried to bring the car to a halt, but it climbed an embankment and blasted through a fence before coming to rest. The fence was lined with spectators, meaning the out-of-control Barracuda struck several people before Petty could get it stopped.

Many were injured and an eight-year-old boy was killed in the accident, leaving Petty, his crew, and of course the child's entire family devastated. The car was parked in the woods behind the Petty shop, where it was eventually buried. Petty does not like to speak of the accident, but he did continue to race afterward in a new Barracuda.

Midway through the 1965 season, NASCAR's Bill France dropped the ban on Hemi engines, so Petty's drag racing career went by the wayside when he got back into the swin of the stock car circuit.

Petty's time behind the wheel of a drag car may hav been short, but he learned a very hard lesson. He drew hug crowds, and put on a great show, but his accident certainly p the dangers of drag racing into perspective. Unfortunately, took a much larger incident to impact the sport in such a man ner that it had no choice but to change.

The Final Straw

Without question, injuries and deaths were not uncon mon in drag racing during the 1950 and 1960s. Crashes we fairly common and mechanical breakage seemed norma

By 1969, funny cars were all the rag and gone were the days of stoc frames and steel bodies. With limite traction and nitro as the fuel of choic early funny cars were nothing short volatile. Huston Platt's *Dixie Twist* Camaro was a fan favorite, but the car wow factor turned tragic at Yellow Riv Drag Strip. (Photo Courtesy Doug Col

March 2, 1969, was a bad day for drag racing; it marked the end of the Yellow River Drag Strip in Covington, Georgia. There would never be another drag car on this historic strip of pavement, as the property was transformed into a mobile home park shortly after the accident.

It was nearly two decades into the sport's legitimized era before tragedy struck in such a manner that forced everyone to take notice.

The venue was Yellow River Drag Strip in Covington, Georgia. Widely known in the Atlanta area as a premier outlaw track, Yellow River had limited safety features, but drew enormous crowds with big-time Funny Car events. Spectators were allowed to roam freely around the facility, sometimes crossing the track on foot between passes. The guardrails at Yellow River were a poor excuse for safety equipment, and they did not extend to the finish line, where containing the vehicle is most crucial. After the 1,000-foot mark, the only thing separating the 200-mph cars from the spectators was an embankment and a hog-wire fence. The lack of guardrails wasn't uncommon at the time, but the fact that the spectators were in such close proximity to the racing surface made it a very treacherous facility.

A fatal crash on March 2, 1969, changed drag racing as we knew it. The day's activities included the regular drag racing program, with the addition of a Funny Car meet. At the time, funny cars were extremely popular, mainly because of the wheelstands, 1,000-foot burnouts, and what seemed to be out-of-control passes down the quarter-mile. This excitement created a sizeable crowd at Yellow River Drag Strip early in the 1969 racing season.

During the event, the track's announcer made an attempt to move the crowds away from the fence, but the thrill of being close to the action was a risk the spectators were willing to take. Fans climbed into the trees surrounding the track to get a better view of the action—the place was packed.

Pulling up to the line was Frank Oglesby, driving "Dyno" Don Nicholson's Mercury Cougar, and Huston Platt, piloting the *Dixie Twister* Camaro. Both cars were very popular nitro-burning funny cars, and the crowd prepared for a great side-by-side pass. Eyes watering from the intense nitro fumes, the spectators close to the start line covered their ears as the cars blasted off the line and down the narrow quarter-mile drag strip. The next thing they heard were horrific screams, as Platt's Camaro careened off the track near the finish line.

Yellow River Drag Strip was the site of an accident that changed drag racing history. Huston Platt's *Dixie Twister* crashed at the top end, killing twelve spectators and injuring many more. This unfortunate event encouraged lawmakers to create guidelines for drag strips, which forced many outlaw tracks out of business. (Photo Courtesy Fred Simmons)

It is reported that Platt lost traction on the unprepared racing surface, and then heard his engine let out a loud explosion, so he instantly shut it down and deployed the parachute to help straighten out the car. What Platt didn't realize was that a spectator had reportedly bent over to pick up his beer just a few feet from the track. The spectator was so close to the track, the Camaro's parachute literally scooped him up, killing him on impact. The additional weight of the man inside the parachute caused Platt's already vulnerable car to veer to the right, off the racing surface and up an embankment before colliding with numerous spectators.

Platt sustained very minimal injuries in the terrible crash, but a total of twelve spectators lost their lives, making this the worst drag racing accident ever recorded in the United States. More than forty spectators were injured, and Platt was later treated for shock, as the reality of the incident set in.

Many accounts of the accident reveal the panic that struck the entire crowd, especially those who had a clear vantage point. The rescue and cleanup efforts were very time-consuming, and many of the spectators left the track in awe of the crash that had taken place. Authorities and track personnel struggled to keep it orderly, encouraging the decision to call off the race and send everyone home. Yellow River Drag Strip was never opened again.

That day scarred the memories of many children an adults in attendance, and it certainly placed a heavy burden c the heart of Huston Platt. Although he continued racing fc a couple more seasons after the crash, Platt realized his racir career would not be remembered for his many victories— would be remembered for the crash at Yellow River. Obv ously, he never enjoyed recalling that day, but he admitte that it made for safer racing. Huston Platt, still a resident c Georgia, passed away on November 30, 2011, at the age of 7

Government officials, as well as a number of leaders in th racing industry knew something had to change to prevent th from happening again. Jim Kaser, director of professional con petition for the Sports Car Club of America (SCCA) state "The accident further emphasizes that operations outside th framework of organized racing are dangerous and should k stopped." Unsanctioned drag strips were soon under seriou scrutiny, meaning they were required to uphold safety sta dards similar to the NHRA- and AHRA-sanctioned tracks c the era. Some tracks were shortened in an effort to make the safer, and many were closed for good because of the unfortu nate accident in Covington, Georgia.

LAKELAND INTERNATIONAL RACEWAY

ot rodders and drag racers in the Memphis, Tennessee, area rejoiced when the airstrip in Halls, Tennessee, became a gitimate place to race. The Rodders Memphis car club, now known as Memphis Rodders, started in 1947 and played big role in the Halls drags, as well as the development of Lakeland Dragway. (Photo Courtesy Marshall Robilio)

Lakeland, Tennessee
1960–1979

Current Status: ➤ **ABANDONED, PARTIALLY REDEVELOPED**

During the drag racing boom in the 1950s, gearheads looked for places to race, and found their answers on abandoned airfields leftover from the war. Countless makeshift drag strips were scattered across the country, and particular airfield kick-started the drag racing scene in the Western portion of Tennessee. Located in Halls, Tennessee, he airfield operated as a drag strip as early as 1955, thanks to he determination of Raymond Godman. A young car guy, Godman became an NHRA Advisor soon after organizing is first race in Halls, and then developed a plan to build a rand-new drag strip closer to Memphis, in the small town of Lakeland, Tennessee.

After a two-year construction process, Lake Land Dragay was opened on July 4, 1960. Much like other drag strips in the area at the time, it was considered state-of-the-art and drew incredible crowds. Godman built and operated the Lake Land track, which eventually used names such as Lakeland International Raceway and Shelby County International Raceway. The reason for the name changes was due to changes in ownership and operations, as the track passed through a few hands during its eighteen-year history. Other big names to operate the track include Bill Taylor, who later made a name for himself in the transmission and torque converter industry—you may have heard of BTE, which stands for Bill Taylor Enterprises.

The 128-acre piece of property offered lots of space for quarter-mile racing, with plenty of room to get stopped. Many national points meets were held at the Lakeland facility

Like most drag strips in the south, Lakeland started small. It was essentially a strip of pavement with a small timing tower and very few amenities. Its location in Memphis made for a huge following of racers, and this photograph depicts a very simple time for the legendary track, which was actually known as Lake Land Dragstrip at the time. (Photo Courtesy LP Photo, Larry Chambers)

The *Coleman-Taylor Automatic Transmissions* dragster is seen here blazing the tires at Lake Land Dragway. The blower and injected small-block Chevy motivated the short-wheelbase dragster during the early 1960s, just a couple of years after the strip opened its doors. Many Memphis-area racers used their drag cars to help draw attention to their businesses. (Photo Courtesy Marshall Robilio)

during its run, with sanctioning coming from all three of the major organizations throughout the years—NHRA, AHRA, and IHRA.

By the late 1960s, Bill Taylor was at the helm of this Memphis-area drag strip, which was in the process of being transformed into a full racing facility, complete with a 1.7-mile road course. Obviously, with only 1.7 miles of real estate on the course, a large portion of it was used for the very long straightaway, so it was a fairly simple layout. By June 1968 the road course was ready for action, and saw its first major event, called the Memphis 200, sanctioned by USAC, a heavy hitter in the stock car industry.

The *Sock It To Me!* big-block injected altered is seen here, rolling into the staging beams at Lakeland International Raceway. Notice the vast improvements in the facility, compared to the early days—the new and improved Lakeland had stylish signage as well as concrete guard walls. (Photo Courtesy LPC Photo, Larry Chambers)

Famous racer Bo Laws makes a hard launch at Lakeland during a big NHRA World Championship event. When the track made changes to include a road course, it also changed its name to Shelby County International Raceway. During the track revamp, a catwalk was added just behind the start line. (Photo Courtesy LPC Photo, Larry Chambers)

This beautiful shot of the *Shreve Automotive* AA/FD dragster seems to really set the mood for the late 1960s drag racing scene. The blown nitro Hemi is belching out flames as it rolls into the beams, while spectators eagerly await the launch. This shot also offers a great view of the new and improved tower. (Photo Courtesy LPC Photo, Larry Chambers)

During this time as a multi-race facility, the track's name was changed to Shelby County International Raceway, but eventually switched back to Lakeland International Raceway. A major milestone for the track was its inclusion in the unforgettable 1971 film, *Two-Lane Blacktop*. This movie is an iconic piece of history for Lakeland, and it plays a large role in people's interest in abandoned drag strips.

For most tracks, the poor economy and lack of interest was enough to force them into retirement, but for Lakeland, that wasn't the case. Even with a shrinking number of racers and spectators, the track trudged on, until the end of the 1978 season, when the owners of a newly developed factory outlet mall terminated the lease. The mall's location was very close to the race track, and there was little to be done to save the track.

For the next few decades the property remained mostly intact, including the walking bridge behind the starting line. The concrete barriers and racing surface remained for quite some time, and even wore the painted-on sponsor logos until the day they were dug up and taken away. The property faced certain death with the city's plans to develop the land near the outlet mall, turning it into a residential area. The intense overgrowth eventually changed the landscape of the facility and major changes to the property, but the memories are strong enough to keep Memphis racers in a state of nostalgia anytime they're in the area.

The hand-painted sponsor signs were still visible when Greg Friend shot these photos more than ten years ago. Although faded and scuffed, these signs are a walk down memory lane for anyone who visited Lakeland International Raceway during its heyday. Many Memphis-based companies advertised on these sacred walls. (Photo Courtesy Greg Friend)

Although heavily overgrown, you can see the hillside that gave spectators a great view of the action. With most of the steel being used for scrap during the dismantling of the track, there isn't much left, aside from the pavement, the concrete walls, and the general landscape of the property. (Photo Courtesy Greg Friend)

More painted signage survives on this stretch of the wall. Racing Head Service (RHS) was yet another Memphis-based company that eventually made it big. RHS is now owned by the Comp Performance Group, which is still based in Memphis. While the paint survives, the weeds and trees have taken over the asphalt racing surface. (Photo Courtesy Greg Friend)

Standing at the finish line and looking toward the starting line, you can see that weeds are taking over the drag strip. Mass overgrowth will eventually swallow the historic race track, but the majority of the property remains intact. (Photo Courtesy Greg Friend)

In 1999, the catwalk was still in place, as the track rested peacefully. It got a rude awakening several years later as further development took place. However, the project was halted, and the track still resides behind a factory outlet mall, which has also been shut down and abandoned. (Photo Courtesy Greg Friend)

GREEN VALLEY RACEWAY

Green Valley Raceway was no backwoods outlaw track. It was a premier track of the South, and attracted thousand of great drag racers to its quarter-mile facility in Smithfield, Texas. Here, the Stone, Woods & Cook Mustang squares o against Arnie Beswick's GTO in a highly anticipated Funny Car match race. (Photo Courtesy Jay S. Magnum)

Smithfield, Texas
1960–1986

Current Status: ➤ **REDEVELOPED INTO SUBDIVISION**

They say everything is bigger in Texas, and in the world of drag racing, this was a very accurate statement. Obviously, the West Coast had a good thing going, but Texas was a major hotspot for drag racing during the 1960s. Legendary racers such as Eddie Hill saw the beginning of Texas drag racing, and they also saw it dwindle as the years rolled on.

There's something to be said for a flagship track and its impact on the drag racing community. For the AHRA, its flagship track in the South was Green Valley Raceway, host of some of the biggest races of the year, with giant turnouts that rivaled those of West Coast tracks. The track never had a sparkling reputation for cleanliness or racer comfort, but it never failed to bring in thousands of folks to watch the racing action.

In the beginning, Green Valley Raceway was nothin more than a dairy farm owned by Bill and Dorothy McClur After taking a flat piece of ground and converting it into drag strip, the McClures had themselves quite the attractio in the small town of Smithfield, Texas. This purpose-bui track opened for business in April 1960, which was durin the NHRA's ban on nitromethane fuel, so McClure opted fo AHRA sanctioning, which meant that the nitro cars coul compete on his quarter-mile track. This approach made Gree Valley Raceway a popular destination for southern racers, an it was especially appealing to spectators, who could expect t see several high-level events each year.

In the heyday of Green Valley Raceway, it was run b renowned track operator Ben Christ, who was a big player i he AHRA. This connection to the AHRA and Christ's vast nowledge of marketing made Green Valley the place to be or drag racing. Even when the NHRA lifted the nitro ban, he AHRA had a strong following of racers so the track continued to prosper into the 1960s. By the mid 1960s, the track ad blossomed into a full-blown raceway park, with a 1.6-mile oad course that used the entire drag strip as the straightaway. Popular road racing organizations, such as the SCCA and its aunted Trans-Am series, ran at Green Valley. After a few races, he creek that ran through the track's property became known s "Mustang Creek," after a crash left a race-prepped Mustang n the drink. The bridge that covered the creek was still intact few years ago, but the area is no longer part of the property.

The track changed hands in 1965, as the McClures moved n to continue with their dairy farm, which was located near he top end of the drag strip. Green Valley continued to oper-

ate under AHRA sanctioning, while new ownership brought a few changes to the track. The new owner was Bill Hielscher, a well-known racer who was also known as "Mr. Bardahl" as he was heavily sponsored by the Bardahl Company. Hielscher's extensive racing background provided a great management strategy throughout his years at the helm.

Even with the change in ownership and management, the track continued to host the biggest national event of the year for the AHRA. Special-event planning made a big impact on the track, with unique events such as an Evel Knievel jump in 1974, which saw the famous daredevil jump eleven Mack trucks on his Harley-Davidson motorcycle. This spectacular event was covered by ABC's *Wide World of Sports*, giving the track a bit of national notoriety that it normally wouldn't have received.

After several more years with lots of big events under the AHRA sanction, Hielscher switched to NHRA sanctioning

The AHRA sanctioned Green Valley and held many big events at the nationally known facility. Funny cars were the big dogs of the sport and always drew a crowd, especially when a bunch of them rolled into town for a national meet. Here, Gene Snow and Mike Burkhart do battle in 1968. (Photo Courtesy Jay S. Magnum)

Green Valley Raceway had lots of room for spectators, which made it a great place for national events. Folks packed the stands and lined up on the catwalk to get a good view of the action. Here is yet another great Funny Car match up—"Dyno Don" and Mr. Norm from 1966. (Photo Courtesy Jay S. Magnum)

This is an interesting shot of Kelly Chadwick's Camaro funny car, taken in 1967. The Dick Harrell signage is taped onto the door, which means that Harrell's car must have suffered a severe breakage the night before. Harrell borrowed Chadwick's car and made his appearance as promised. (Photo Courtesy Jay S. Magnum)

in 1977. Eventually, he renamed the track Green Valley Race City but for most folks, the drag strip is remembered as Green Valley Raceway or simply "the Valley." While NHRA Division 4 races were held at Green Valley in the late 1970s and early 1980s, the track had lost some of its momentum, like so many tracks during the era. However, it survived the toughest times and made it to 1986, when the track finally shut down

The tower at Green Valley always stood out with its black-and-white checkerboard paint scheme, but the tower did move from one side of the track to the other on a few occasions. The covered bleachers and catwalk were also big features of the track, but most people remember it for the cars. (Photo Courtesy Jay S. Magnum)

for good. At the time of closure, the facility had certainly seen better days, and the growing population of the North Richland Hills area contributed to the situation.

During the years after closing the track Hielscher ran Amarillo Dragway for a short time, and then bought Texas Raceway in Kennedale, Texas. He passed away several years ago, leaving his daughter to run the race track. Even after its closure, Green Valley remained mostly intact for several years. The buildings remained in place, as did the racing surface, but the grandstands, sound system, and other usable items were repurposed. The track was later used as a testing area for "toll tags," which are currently in use in the Dallas area.

By the late 1990s, surrounding neighborhoods grew closer and closer to the abandoned race track, and developers overtook the land completely by 2005. Clearing the land of all its artifacts and completely changing the layout of the area meant that old-time racers may not even recognize the grounds when passing through, as roads have been re-routed to cater to the community. A small portion of the shutdown area pavement, however, remains on an untouched part of the property, so a small sliver of the track's twenty-five-year history lives on in this hallowed ground. With houses scattered across the land that was once an AHRA flagship track, there's very little remaining of one of the most famous drag strips in the South

Unfortunately, this is all that remains of the legendary Green Valley Raceway facility. After the track closed in 1986, it sat vacant for several years, until developers chose to use the land for a new subdivision. The original pavement still resides on both sides of the subdivision, but there isn't much left of it. (Photo Courtesy Steve Scott)

This concrete bridge is still intact, even after the major land development in 2005. The creek by the bridge was located behind the starting line. This portion of the track, as well as a small part of the pits, is still intact on one side of the subdivision. (Photo Courtesy Steve Scott)

On the other side of the subdivision is the finish line and shutdown area, which saw some serious action in the old days. Green Valley had huge vertical boards at the finish line, which were sponsored by Sprite, and gave the track a well-known characteristic—almost as memorable as the checkered timing tower. (Photo Courtesy Steve Scott)

Dallas International Motor Speedway looked to be a major player in the drag racing and road racing world, but a terrible string of bad luck left it in sad shape shortly after its grand opening. During its good times, the track was one of the greats, but the good times just didn't last. (Photo Courtesy David Graves)

Dallas, Texas
1969–1973

Current Status: ➤ **REDEVELOPED A. LARGE RETAIL COMPLEX**

In the heyday of drag racing, hometown tracks were the norm, even for big-time racers. However, by the late 1960s, it had become apparent that this drag racing thing was a profitable market, so land developers and investors began sinking more money into drag strip construction. This resulted in several high-level tracks that catered to very large national events. One of these purpose-built tracks was Dallas International Motor Speedway (DIMS), with its high-tech construction and multi-use capabilities. It opened in 1969 with high hopes of becoming one of the nation's top tracks right off the bat.

While it did have a big turnout for the NHRA Spring Nationals (its first major event), tragedy struck on that day. Funny Car eliminations saw Pat Foster go head-to-head with Gerry Schwartz in round one, but a horrific crash put a damper on the day's competition. Foster spun the tires down track, and crossed the centerline, where Schwartz was barreling ahead in his Chevy-powered Cougar. While Foster took a hard hit, it was Schwartz who suffered severe injuries, which

claimed his life before arriving at the hospital. This crash was a bad way to start the track's short-lived career, and things didn't get any better.

With big plans for the 1970 season, the DIMS crew had been awarded two of the four NHRA national events, as well as an SCCA Trans-Am series race, scheduled for late April. Although lots of planning gave the crew motivation early in the year, success just wasn't meant to be for this Texas track. Torrential downpours halted a number of events, including the Trans-Am race, to be held on the 2½-mile road course. Unfortunately, Trans-Am never rescheduled the event.

During all the rain, the property suffered flood damage, and with each weekend that went by without a major event, the financial burden became more of an issue. Making matters even worse, the property's neighbors began complaining, which resulted in a track curfew of 10:00 pm. All of these factors played major roles in the track's demise, but the bad news doesn't stop there.

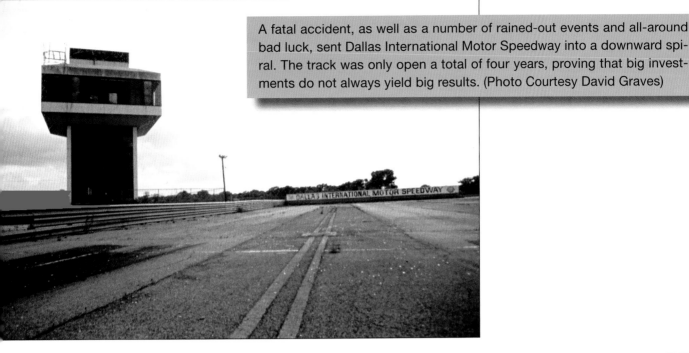

A fatal accident, as well as a number of rained-out events and all-around bad luck, sent Dallas International Motor Speedway into a downward spiral. The track was only open a total of four years, proving that big investments do not always yield big results. (Photo Courtesy David Graves)

Even with all of these unfortunate events, the track management pressed on and hoped to bring renewed success. The decision was made to switch sanctioning bodies for the 1971 season, so DIMS converted its operations to the IHRA rulebook, looking for a better deal. The NHRA's requirement was 50 percent of the gate, while IHRA sanctioning required only a 25-percent cut, so track management had chosen to change sanctioning bodies in an effort to save every dollar they could. Try as they might, though, the money situation didn't seem to improve over the next two years of operation.

Another tragic event occurred in October 1971 as Gene Thomas, a Dallas news reporter, spent the day at DIMS doing a story on the track. He strapped into Art Arfons' *Super Cyclops* jet car, which was equipped with two seats. A brave man to even think about going for a ride in this 280-mph jet car, Thomas was involved in a crash that claimed his life, as well as the lives of two spectators. Arfons, the legendary jet-car racer, retired from drag racing after the horrific incident.

After only a few years of operation, Dallas International Motor Speedway closed its doors. Financial trouble and an unbelievable string of bad luck spelled major trouble for the high-dollar drag strip, and 1973 marked the end of its very short life. After its closure, the property sat unused for many years. It was later sold to land developers and restructured into a large retail complex, which completely masked the fact that the track ever existed.

The demise of this track was caused by several factors, but the expansion of the Dallas area would've been troublesome to the track regardless of its accident record. Now, racers can only think back to the times when DIMS was a strong force in the Dallas area, and wonder how it all would've shaken out if luck had been on its side.

The tower at DIMS was a work of art, so it was certainly a shame to let it go to waste. It stood abandoned for a few years, but the entire facility was later sold to land developers and transformed into a large retail complex. (Photo Courtesy David Graves)

HUDSON DRAG STRIP

Located in the small town of Hudson, North Carolina, the track known as Hudson Drag Strip was home to many grea[t] of the sport. Although the track never really got the recognition it deserved, it is certainly remembered now that it is n[o] longer in operation. The track was carved out of the mountainous terrain and survived from 1959 to 1994. (Photo Cou[r]tesy Van Abernethy)

Hudson, North Carolina
1959-1994

Current Status: ➤ **ABANDONE[D]**

North Carolina is known for its mountainous terrain, so finding a flat piece of land proved to be quite difficult for drag strip entrepreneurs in the late 1950s. A strip of land was carved out of a hillside to create enough level real estate to hold a drag race, but the rest of the land had some unique characteristics because of the hilly landscape. Hudson Drag Strip is a prime example of a drag strip that was built in an area that honestly didn't have enough room for a drag strip. It was built and owned by George Shell on a piece of property that was anything but flat.

Shell moved enough dirt to create a flat racing surface and opened Hudson Drag Strip in June 1959. It was originally a dirt drag strip, which was actually quite common in North Carolina, but it was paved only a few months after its grand opening. The response to this new drag strip was huge, so a continuing effort to improve the facility kept Shell quite busy.

He had help from locals Earl Shell, Jay McLean, and Cle[m] Sullivan in the early days, and was committed to being op[en] every Sunday of the year, weather permitting.

Cars came from all around to race at Hudson, sometim[e] from the mountains with snow still on their vehicles. Coff[ee] was a popular item at the concession stand during those har[sh] winter months. However, being open every weekend ha[d] advantages when it came to racer and spectator awareness—they didn't have to ask around to find out if Hudson was op[en] because of the track's reputation for year-round racing.

Many drag strips built in the 1950s and 1960s had uphi[ll] shutdown areas, but Hudson took the cake with what wa[s] essentially a mountainside for a shutdown area. The stee[p] grade was great for the extremely fast cars, because it too[k a] lot of effort to run off the end of the track. The hilly landscap[e] also played into the spectator seating, as the land to the rig[ht]

While the right side of the track was essentially a large bank with bleachers, the left side had a sizeable timing tower and concession stand, along with the pits. Multiple houses (one can be seen in the distance) were located very close to the drag strip; it would never pass the noise ordinances of today. (Photo Courtesy Van Abernethy)

side of the track was much higher than on the left side. Spectators could look down on the action from the right side, while the pit side (left) was actually lower than the track.

While most tracks had poor restroom facilities and concessions, Hudson Drag Strip had a fairly nice setup. The word on the street is that Hudson hot dogs were mighty good. After the good ol' days of gassers, altereds, and super stockers had passed, the track became a hotspot for Pro Stock racing. In the early 1970s, the track was leased by Tom Ferrell, who continued to operate the track for seven years. During that time, dedicated Pro Stock meets were popular events, so Ferrell held these heads-up races to keep up with demand.

When Ferrell didn't renew his lease for the 1980 season, the track sat unused for a year. Still, it wasn't a fearful time for the North Carolina racers, even though many big tracks were closing their doors forever. Hudson Drag Strip came back in 1981 with new ownership and big plans to renovate the track. By the 1983 racing season, concrete had been poured for a brand-new starting-line area, which greatly increased traction and offered a solid foundation that held up to lots of abuse.

This photo from the burnout box area shows the extreme grade of the bank on the right side of the track. You can also see the proximity of houses to the roaring drag strip, which prided itself on being open every weekend of the year, even the winter. (Photo Courtesy Van Abernethy)

Hudson Drag Strip had concrete guard walls, but spectators on the pit side were allowed to get very close to the action. Hudson was home to a big heads-up drag racing scene, and gave traction to a lot of racers who wanted to go fast but didn't have a professional class in which to run. (Photo Courtesy Van Abernethy)

This view of the track provides another glimpse at the very steep spectator area, which was extremely dangerous. One wrong move and you could potentially roll down the embankment and onto the track. Notice that there were no guard-rails on the right side of the track. (Photo Courtesy Van Abernethy)

he old ticket booth at the gate can still be found at the udson Drag Strip. The "Glass Bottles Prohibited" sign as fallen off the building. It's amazing that no one has ken it for a souvenir, but the entire track seems to be ntouched since its final race in 1994.

More signs that the track has been left untouched all these years is the wiring system, speakers, and lights. When most tracks are closed permanently, equipment is either reused at another facility or hauled off for scrap. At Hudson Drag Strip, everything is still there, just as it was in 1994.

tense overgrowth has turned this drag strip into a very eerie place. The bleachers are completely consumed by the ees and weeds; the pit side of the track is equally overgrown. However, the track surface appears to be in decent nape, as the concrete starting line was only a few years old at the time of closing.

These improvements came at a time when pro stock cars were really pushing the limits of the rulebooks, which forced many racers into match races when they could no longer pass tech for the class. Super-lightweight cars with big-displacement mountain engines became the norm for those outlaw pro stock cars, and the high demand for quicker and faster doorslammers created a new class in drag racing. Today, we call it Pro Modified (Pro Mod), but back then it was just all-out heads-up racing, and as long as the car had functioning doors, it was okay to race.

The heyday of Pro Mod was most certainly the 1980s and early 1990s, as wild car designs made them fan favorites in the pits, while the wild rides and crazy driving jobs offered plenty of excitement on the track. Hudson was a hotspot for Pro Mod racing, which is fitting because the entire state of North Carolina had a big following for the class.

As the years roll on, the class has evolved tremendously, with cars that are unbelievably fast, but lack the individual personality that 1990s-era Pro Mods were known for. Back then, a nitrous purge and a few good dry hops brought a crowd to its feet, then left them amazed when the driver zinged the engine, popped the clutch, and pulled those Lenco levers like there was no tomorrow.

Hudson Drag Strip eventually met its demise in 19** when a property disagreement finally reached its boili** point. The heated family feud resulted in a small portic** of the property not being leased by its owner. This ma** it impossible for the track to run, so at the end of t** 1994 season, Hudson Drag Strip closed its doors, never reopen again.

The owners simply left the track as it was on the fin** day. No upkeep, no demolition, and no action has result** in a very somber reminder of a historic Southern race trac** The bleachers, restrooms, buildings, and fences are still place, but badly damaged by the lack of attention.

The strip of pavement is in surprisingly good sha** after all these years, but the buildings are barely able to ho** their own weight. With widespread overgrowth, weeds a** trees are abundant, but it's painfully obvious that this pla** was once a hotbed for drag racing, right up to its final eve** in 1994. While it never had the celebrity status of the We** Coast's super tracks, it certainly put a fire under thousan** of North Carolina racers and fans after nearly four decad** of operation. There is no hope in bringing back Hudso** Drag Strip, but its remains stand as a memorial to the go** times had at one of the hilliest drag strips in America.

The restrooms are still intact atop the hill on the right side of the track. They are now essentially located in someone** back yard. All of the buildings at the old Hudson Drag Strip are still standing—it's as if the owners simply turned out th** lights and walked away.

n the pit side, a clearing provides an open shot at the timing tower and concession stand. A quick look inside the ilapidated buildings didn't yield any interesting artifacts, but you can bet there was plenty of cool stuff left behind when e track closed. Most of the pit area is now overtaken by trees.

n old Pepsi sign still hangs on the front side of the concession stand, which faced the drag strip, but most other sigage has fallen off after years of neglect. The roofs of the bathrooms, timing tower, and concession stand are in poor nape, but all of the buildings are still upright.

SHUFFLETOWN DRAGWAY

With Pro Modified racing as its claim to fame, Shuffletown Dragway also served as a great place for regular bracket racing, as well as a place for street cars to legally do battle. This shot offers a good view of the timing tower, which is still standing today. (Photo Courtesy David Smith)

Charlotte, North Carolina
1959–1992

Current Status: ➤ **ABANDONED ADJACENT TO A PUBLIC PARK**

Shuffletown Dragway is one of many abandoned race tracks in the Southeast that happens to be placed in one of the most racing-oriented cities in America—Charlotte, North Carolina. There are many interesting things in the history of Shuffletown, including the community it was named after and the track's thirty-three-year timeline. Shuffletown, slightly northwest of Charlotte, was a small community of farmers. The entire town consisted of a country store, a couple of gas stations, and a river ferry—but no longer exists.

The Shuffletown area definitely had character, and a drag strip only added to the small-town flavor, especially during the first few years of operation. The idea to build a drag strip was a ploy by the Charlotte Police Department to get hot rodders off the streets, giving them a legal place to race. The drag strip needed to be easily accessible from Charlotte, but not placed too close to town or suburban areas, which made Shuffletown the perfect location.

The plot of land was located near a creek, so it was already fairly level, and by 1959 the land had a clean straight away of packed dirt. Racing began that year on the dirt strip which offered plenty of excitement, even for stock street cars of the era. The loose surface presented quite the challenge, but Shuffletown Dragway remained in its all-dirt configuration until 1964.

Charlotte was already a hotspot for round-track racing by 1964, and the reconfiguration of Shuffletown Dragway drew even larger crowds of racers and spectators. The track was originally run as a fifth-mile track (1,056 feet), but even with this shorter-than-standard racing distance, it suffered from a short shutdown area. Many top-end crashes and near misses were a result of the abbreviated shutdown length, which eventually led to a creek. As the years passed, cars continued to get faster, so the track was shortened to an eighth mile (660 feet) to provide a few hundred more feet of shutdown area.

Although Shuffletown Dragway had a long career as Charlotte's premier drag strip, it exploded in popularity during the late 1980s and early 1990s. During this time, heads-up drag racing was very popular, and the evolving group of high-end doorslammers created a class that we now call Pro Modified. (Photo Courtesy Van Abernethy)

Shuffletown had a great following in the early days, with a number of big events at the narrow and short eighth-mile track. Steel guardrails with wooden posts lined both sides of the track, while a chain-link fence protected spectators but kept them plenty close to the action. (Photo Courtesy Van Abernethy)

The 1955 Chevy in the near lane is none other than Charles Carpenter, one of the forefathers of Pro Modified drag racing. Starting as a Top Sportsman Quick-8 type of event, it quickly grew into its own class, with drivers such as Scotty Cannon and Rob Vandergriff coming onto the scene with big-inch engines and lots of nitrous. (Photo Courtesy Van Abernethy)

The remains of Shuffletown Dragway are accessible to the public, with the old strip now adjacent to a public park. The track can be seen from Bellhaven Boulevard, but most of it is drastically overgrown. Part of the parking and pit area are still visible, and some staging lane markers can still be seen on the pavement.

The track's concrete starting line is still in fair shape, but the construction of a neighboring park ruined most of the asphalt surface down track. Just past the finish line, a large pile of dirt and sand is conveniently placed to prevent folks from driving onto the old strip.

Lots of big doorslammer races were held at Shuffletown during the mid to late 1960s, and it was home to a huge match race in 1969 between legends Don Garlits and "TV Tommy" Ivo. Another highlight from 1969 is when "Ohio George" Montgomery came to Shuffletown with his twin turbo Boss Mustang. The car was way ahead of its time, and proved to be too powerful for the racing surface, as the Mustang veered out of control and crashed badly. George escaped the crash without serious injury, as did many others. Reportedly, Shuffletown Dragway never had a fatal accident in all of its years of competition, which is something few drag strips can claim.

One interesting aspect of Shuffletown Dragway is that it advertised drag racing fifty-two weeks a year in the 1970s. The weather had to be very poor for management to cancel a race day, so it was a great place to test during the winter months.

The extra shutdown area came in quite handy in the 1980s, as Shuffletown became a popular destination for Pro Modified racing. These very powerful doorslammers were always on the ragged edge, and getting them stopped was just as difficult; racers pulled their parachutes as they passed the first MPH cone (66 feet away from the actual finish line) so they could be fully blossomed just past the stripe.

This new class of cars offered close racing and wild action, and it all started because of a few outlaw doorslammers from the South. Charles Carpenter in his "world's fastest 1955 Chevy" faced off against Jim Bryant's "world's fastest 1957 Chevy" in numerous match races across the country. These wild cars created quite a stir in the industry, and by 1989, Pro Mod was an official class in the IHRA. Many say that Pro Modified racing started at Shuffletown because it was Pro Mod pioneer Charles Carpenter's home track.

Shuffletown had a great following of drag racers and spectators, as it was a sister track to nearby Mooresville Dragway, which ran on Saturday nights. Shuffletown ran on Sunday, so racers could compete at both tracks on the same weekend. Mooresville Dragway is still in operation and holds a Shuffletown tribute race every year.

One of the old scoreboards is still standing on the right side of the track. Most artifacts on the left side of the track were disposed of during construction of a park, leaving the right side as it was when the track closed in 1992 due to the property being annexed into the city of Charlotte.

The timing tower is barely standing on its own, and almost all of the siding has been ripped off during the track's abandonment. The area behind the tower is impassible due to the overgrowth, but many areas of the track are clear enough to do some exploring, especially in winter.

When Shuffletown Dragway's time came to an end, it wasn't because of low attendance. It was because of noise ordinances, which were enforced when the Shuffletown community was annexed into the city of Charlotte in the early 1990s. The track closed in 1992, and sat vacant for many years until a new park was built on part of the track's property. The new Shuffletown Park is a great place for car guys to visit because the remains of Shuffletown Dragway are within walking distance, and there are no posted signs to keep folks off the property. Not much remains of the historic North Carolina track, but it's easy to imagine the good ol' days of this strip just by walking the badly weathered remnants.

Most abandoned drag strips have been completely cleared of artifacts, either by the property owners or by locals who want to take home a little piece of racing history. Along with the remains of Shuffletown Dragway, there are a number of racing slicks scattered around the property, such as these old Firestones.

All of the steel guardrails have been removed from the track, but the wooden posts are still driven into the ground. During exploration of the track, I only found one piece of the track's guardrailing, which was known for its signature white-and-red paint scheme.

CHAPTER 1

CHATTANOOGA HOTSPOTS

During the drag racing boom of the 1950s and 1960s, drag strips popped up all over the place. Big cities, suburban areas, and tiny towns had their own drag strips, so it was possible for racers to compete at a variety of tracks without traveling very far. I'll call it a "drag racing hub," where racers could travel 100 miles or less in any direction and come across well over a dozen places to race. There were many hubs across the country, but the one focused on here is around Chattanooga, Tennessee. There were also numerous choices in northern Tennessee, as well as a plethora of tracks in northeast Alabama and northern Georgia. Each track had its own personality and catered to a diverse group of cars. Some tracks were large enough to attract the big names of the sport, while others kept it simple with their own brew of homegrown drag racing classes.

The West Coast guys might have had Southerners covered on track quality, but this particular drag racing hub won the battle of quantity with a total of fifteen tracks within a 100-mile radius of Chattanooga.

In the 1960s, the big-time racers didn't mind traveling for days to attend a national event, but the low-buck guys usually stayed fairly close to home. That example of a 100-mile radius made for a two-hour trip to the track in most cases, so it wasn't a very long haul. Most guys at small-town tracks couldn't afford to haul their cars on a fancy ramp truck or a trailer, so it was quite normal to see a gasser being flat towed behind a clapped-out pickup truck or station wagon. Put another way, if you pulled up to the track with your car on a trailer, you obviously had a "big money operation." Of course, all of this changed as time went on, but it was a pretty big deal in the early days.

Sticking close to home was never an option for the well-known racers, because the real money could be found only at national events and well-promoted match races. But small tracks were notorious for drawing a big crowd for a match race—it was the modern-day equivalent of having Tony Schumacher and Larry Dixon in a Top Fuel match race at your hometown track today. That stuff just doesn't happen

The South was home to some of the most unsafe drag racing in the country, but this level of danger is what kept folks coming back on a regular basis. The lack of guardrails or any other form of safety equipment didn't keep racers or spectators from supporting their local tracks. (Photo Courtesy Larry Rose Collection)

ere is Peewee Wallace in the *Virginian* altered-wheelase Mopar at Paradise Drag Strip. Notice that there are o spectators in the photo, as Wallace made this exhiition pass specifically for the photographer, who had ttended the Georgia outlaw A/FX event. (Photo Courtesy alter Parsons)

anymore, but in the 1950s, 1960s, and 1970s, racers were not opposed to putting it all on the line under what we now consider dangerous circumstances. Many small-town tracks didn't have guardrails, safety/medical personnel, or a particularly good racing surface, so turning a nitro-injected drag car loose didn't always end well. It may have been exciting but that doesn't mean it was safe.

There were a great number of cities where drag racing was plentiful, but the example of Chattanooga, Tennessee, was chosen here because of its popular location and great mix of racing action. The little tracks in this area didn't hold a candle to the likes of Lions, U.S. 30, or Gainesville, but they meant the world to the folks who raced there so many years ago. It would be a shame to bypass these smaller tracks, when there is a wealth of information, pictures, and stories to be shared.

ust south of Chattanooga, Tennessee, the town of Dalton, Georgia, had its own drag strip, which consisted of a acked-dirt racing surface. It is seen here with a Buick versus Desoto battle taking the stage. These cars appear to be tock, but you can bet the dirt surface made it exciting! (Photo Courtesy Larry Rose Collection)

he outlaw atmosphere is something that most other regions couldn't replicate and it made for some of the greatest acing in the sport. Although poor track conditions often resulted in tire spin farther down the track, you could usually ount on a wheels-up start from the big name cars such as "Dyno" *Don's Eliminator II* Comet in the far lane at Yellow iver Drag Strip in Covington, Georgia. (Photo Courtesy Fred Simmons)

Chattanooga Update

With such a rich history, and a huge following of racers and spectators, the Chattanooga, Tennessee, area suffered a great loss when various drag strips began closing. For years, the limited selection of drag strips caused a lack of interest, which certainly didn't help the hobby. In this particular area, most of the tracks closed prior to the economic down-turn of the late 1970s. Many of these tracks were small, outlaw operations with very little safety equipment, so the Yellow River crash in 1969 made it tough for the track owners to continue operating on the edge. Many factors went into the decreasing size of this particular drag racing hotspot, and the same can be said of other regions in the country.

By the end of the 1990s, former racers were eager to catch up with their drag racing buddies, so reunion events began to pop up around the region. Not long after, a few drag strips began having nostalgia drag events, which prompted many retired racers to bring out their vintage machinery for all to see. Most of the nostalgia events are held at historic tracks. The young racers love seeing the diverse cars, while the drag racing veterans relive the good old days, with gassers, front-engine dragsters, and funny cars blasting down the track.

All of the Chattanooga-area tracks that are still in operation have been shortened to eighth-mile lengths, but the nostalgia racing is fun to watch, regardless of the distance. It pays tribute to the racers and the cars of yesteryear, while offering a fun atmosphere for everyone involved.

After a few decades of racing without many of the Chattanooga area tracks, several drag strips began promoting nostalgia drag events on a regular basis. Paradise Drag Strip in Calhoun, Georgia, has two major nostalgia meets per year, which brings out a great crowd of vintage drag cars, such as this wheelstanding front-engine dragster.

Paradise Drag Strip is still going strong, even after more than fifty years in operation. Along with the nostalgia events, Paradise runs a weekly bracket-racing program on Sunday afternoons. Even with track improvements, Paradise still has the vintage feel with its uphill burnout area and old-school timing tower.

Although it is a little out of the 100-mile range, 411 Dragway in Seymour, Tennessee, holds at least one nostalgia drag event per year. Unfortunately, recent tribulations between property owners and the track management have put a damper on the track's future, despite many efforts to keep it alive.

BRAINERD OPTIMIST CLUB DRAG STRIP

When the Brainerd Optimist Club Drag Strip opened, the races were held north of Chattanooga, in the small town of Hixson. Complaining neighbors forced the club to move its operations to a new facility in 1964. Here, a heavily channeled 1932 Ford coupe lines up against a home-built dragster as the flagman gives them the signal. (Photo Courtesy Larry Rose Collection)

Distance from Chattanooga, 18 Miles
1957–1964

Current Status: ➤ **DALLAS BAY SKYPARK AIRPORT**

In the late 1950s drag strips were few and far between in the South. The West Coast guys were ahead of the game, but it didn't take long for the gearheads back East to follow suit. Many towns had the necessary land for a drag strip, but Hixson was one of the first drag strips in the area. John "Buddy" Houts is responsible for presenting the idea to city and county officials, and he decided it would be best if the proceeds benefited a local charity. The Brainerd Optimist Club jumped at the opportunity.

The drag strip featured a huge expanse of pavement, 3,160 feet long and 40 feet wide. A story ran in the *Chattanooga News Free Press* stating, "Beasts will roar every Sunday on Drag Strip built by Brainerd Optimists with police okay." Trees were cleared, the land was leveled, and asphalt was poured before being sanctioned by the Automobile Timing Association of America and fitted with electronic timing equipment. The Brainerd Optimist Club invested $20,000 to build the track, and opened it to the public on August 11, 1957.

On that summer day, more than 5,000 spectators entered the Brainerd Optimist Club Drag Strip, paying an admission fee of 90 cents. Children under twelve were allowed to enter free of charge. This was a big event. After only thirty days of operation, the newspaper reported that one hundred neighbors of the drag strip had banded together to hire an attorney, because the track "has shattered the peace and quietude of the area."

Night racing stared in 1960, which increased car and spectator counts. The Brainerd Optimist Club began looking for a new piece of property after a few years of constant complaining from the locals. In 1964, the drag strip was converted into the Dallas Bay Skypark, which is still in operation today and the Brainerd Optimist Club moved its drag strip operation to a new facility in Ringgold, Georgia.

After the drag strip operation moved to Ringgold, Georgia, in 1964, the giant strip of pavement was converted into a small airport—Dallas Bay Skypark. The beautiful piece of property doesn't have any drag racing artifacts on it, but the underlying pavement definitely has a story to tell.

Fast forward a few decades and Brainerd still has the same look. The old control tower on the left was torn down prior to the 2012 season and replaced with a new building in a different location. The new management team did lots of work to prepare the track for serious racing action.

Distance from Chattanooga, 10 Miles

1964–Current

Current Status: ➤ 1/8-MILE UNSANCTIONED DRAG STRIP

After moving to this brand-new facility in Ringgold in 1964, the Brainerd Optimist Club continued to support the Chattanooga area drag racing scene. The new track was conveniently located right off Interstate 75. The only problem with the location was the fact that the property is in a low-lying area near a large creek. What eventually became known simply as "Brainerd," the drag strip was a huge success in its early days.

Throughout the 1960s and 1970s, Brainerd flourished and kept a steady flow of racers and spectators coming through the gate on a weekly basis. Moving into the 1980s, Brainerd carried lots of momentum as one of the great tracks in the Southeast. Large pits, good seating, and a well-prepped racing surface made it a great place to race. The IHRA selected it as home to one of its national points meets. Originally a quarter-mile drag strip, Brainerd was one of many tracks shortened to an eighth mile due to increased safety regulations.

Although dark and grainy, this shot from atop the hill at Brainerd shows the track in the 1970s. At that time, the track was run as a full quarter-mile track, but was shortened in the 1980s due to safety concerns. It still runs as an eighth-mile track with a lengthy shutdown area. (Photo Courtesy Richard McFalls)

During the early 1990s, the track went through a few changes and operations were eventually taken over by a new lessee, Steve Longley. He was one of the first track promoters to offer a large purse and a somewhat organized rule set for outlaw street car racing.

By 2005, the outlaw scene had outgrown Brainerd, so it was back to index and bracket racing at the historic track. At the end of the 2011 racing season, the Brainerd Optimist Club again took over operations from Steve and his crew after seventeen years of hard work.

In the past decade, the track has been completely under water several times, damaging the racing surface as well as the buildings on the property. The buildings were repaired, but the pavement is not up to the standards of ten years ago. Big changes may be in store for what is certainly Chattanooga, Tennessee's hometown track.

PARADISE DRAG STRIP

Paradise Drag Strip in Calhoun, Georgia, was one of the finest representations of Southern drag racing you will find. In this shot spectators line the wooden guardrails, while two A/FX cars leave the line. That's Howard Neal driving the *Strip Teaser* in the far lane, with Robert Nance piloting the *Mr. Plymouth* in the near lane. (Photo Courtesy Ronnie Evans)

Distance from Chattanooga, 10 Miles
1961–Current

Current Status: ➤ 1/8-MILE UNSANCTIONED DRAG STRIP

When Paradise Drag Strip was built in 1961, it already had some competition to the north and to the south of Calhoun, Georgia, but its owner and founder, Otto Timms, felt confident that it was a necessary addition to his community. He was a hard worker, and kept his day job while he built the track and ran the operation. Throughout the years, one thing was certain—if you visited Paradise Drag Strip you would see Otto in the pits or on the track. He was truly in his element, even into his elder years, when Alzheimer's disease began to degrade his health.

Starting in 1961, Paradise Drag Strip was a hotspot for Super Stock drag racing. The quarter-mile track was narrow and featured shin-high wooden guardrails. Among many track improvements over the years, Otto added a unique timing tower between the racing lanes, just before the starting

line. Another interesting feature of Paradise Drag Strip is its uphill burnout box and its slightly uphill starting line. An uphill shutdown area made for safe stops in most cases, but the track was eventually shortened to eighth-mile, just like all of the other unsanctioned tracks in the area.

Racing activity took a hit in the later years at Paradise, but a revived interest from the nostalgia drag racing crowd brought spectators to the track a few times a year. With the majority of regular bracket races occurring on Sunday, Otto always had a strict rule that no cars could be started until church let out across the street.

Otto Timms passed away in his home at approximately 2:00 pm on February 27, 2011, during a regular Sunday bracket race at Paradise. His family had always been a big help at Paradise, so they continued operation of the track, paying tribute to the man who built it with his own hands and ran it for fifty years. His wife, Carol, along with their children and grandchildren, still work at Paradise, but it will never be the same without Otto.

Your eyes aren't fooling you—the starting line at Paradise Drag Strip is not level. In fact, any manual-transmission cars without a line-lock rolls out of the beams if the driver isn't paying attention. Paradise is still in good working order, and holds several nostalgia drag events each year.

DOUBLE H DRAG STRIP

Although it was a long drive with the mountainous terrain and poor roads, Blue Ridge, Georgia, had a great drag stri just outside town. The *Strip Teaser* Thunderbolt is certainly the star of this photo, but check out that Corvair suppo truck! (Photo Courtesy Ronnie Evans)

Distance from Chattanooga, **82 Miles** *1963-1966* Current Status: ➤ **BLUE RID SKYPORT AIRPO**

A lack of flat ground didn't deter Bill Hembree from building a drag strip on the outskirts of Blue Ridge, Georgia. Constructed in 1963, Double H never had guardrails, but this outlaw atmosphere is what made Southeastern drag racing so popular. During its prime time, Double H Drag Strip hosted a number of match races, along with its regular Gas classes and a special class called "Cheatin' Four Barrel," which was designed for cars that didn't quite meet the requirements for the Gas classes.

Double H never had a Christmas tree, always relying on a flagman to start the race. A small timing tower was located on the left side of the track, while the right side was the spectator area. The shutdown area was uphill, and featured a turnaround at the end, meaning the racers had to drive backward on the track, until a very narrow return road began near the actual finish line. It was certainly a unique facility.

The Grand Opening was held on November 17, 1963, but the biggest moment for Double H Drag Strip came on Sunday, May 9, 1965, when it was the third and final track in a grueling three-day, three-track Super Stock event called

the World Series of Drag Racing. A purse of $1,000 per da was up for grabs, so racers came from as far away as Detroi New York, and Louisiana to compete at Paradise Drag Str on Friday night, Brainerd Optimist Drag Strip on Saturda night, and then Double H Drag Strip on Sunday afternoo The three rules for this huge Super Stock event were: Th cars must weigh no less than 3,200 pounds, have an unalter wheelbase, and have an engine no larger than 427 ci.

Shortly after this big event, the track faced hard tim and operations were eventually transferred to Harold Mille At this time, the track's name changed to Lost Mounta Drag Strip but it didn't last much longer after that. A li tle over a decade ago, the property was sold and the ne owner, James Clack, added to the existing asphalt to create runway for private use. He calls it the Blue Ridge Skypo The new owner says that he lets some of his local gearhe friends make "passes" on the abandoned drag strip, so yc can bet the spirit of the track is still alive and well, ev though the last legitimate pass down Double H Drag Str was in 1966.

SOUTHEASTERN INTERNATIONAL DRAGWAY

One of Georgia's first drag strips, Southeastern International Dragway, had a prime location—it was accessible by the Chattanooga crowd and also very close to Atlanta. The track opened in 1955, and grew into a major destination by the late 1960s and early 1970s, with big events on a regular basis. (Photo Courtesy Fred Simmons)

Distance from Chattanooga, 95 Miles
1955-2005

Current Status: ➤
ABANDONED

The oldest drag strip in this drag racing hub is Southeastern International Dragway. Opened on July 4, 1955, and known as "Red's Drag Strip," this track was owned and operated by Marvin "Red" Jones and located in Dallas, Georgia, northwest of Atlanta. The original drag strip consisted of a tar-and-gravel surface, with a racing length of 1,000 feet. A few years after opening, the drag strip was reconfigured to include an improved racing surface, but the old portion of the track still remained as the return road. At this time, the track was lengthened to a full quarter mile.

On January 1, 1963, Charles Hardy took over operations, a big step up from his former job as flagman. Hardy's family members helped run the track for quite some time. Moving into the heyday of Super Stock racing, Hardy had a great location and facility for big events, so it was common to see a huge turnout of well-known drivers at Southeastern International Dragway.

By 1966, the NHRA jumped on board to sanction the track, and actually held its Division 2 finals at Southeastern, with a packed house. Later in the 1960s, the track became a hotspot for Funny Car races, but it was decided to shorten the racing distance to 1,000 feet. All other classes were still allowed to run the full quarter. Eventually the track was shortened to an eighth mile, much like the other tracks in the area. A brand-new concrete racing surface revitalized the historic track in the 1990s.

Gene Fuller took over as track manager, and helped boost the track's popularity with cool class structures and interesting events. He promoted the track until its last event on December 11, 2005. The reason for closing was simple—the land had been bought and plans were made to develop it. Unfortunately for the new owners, the ground didn't pass water dissipation/percolation testing, so local ordinances did not approve building permits and they were unable to build on the property.

The concession stand and bathrooms still stand, but the tower has been burned to the ground and all of the guardrails and bleachers have been scrapped. The racing surface is still intact, but due to the change in ownership, it can no longer be grandfathered into the local ordinances to operate as a drag strip.

Georgia drag racing legend Shirl Greer (near lane) leaves the line at Southeastern in his *Tension* funny car. Notice th the track has a bit of a crown and an un-level starting line, similar to Paradise Drag Strip. Both Paradise and Southeas ern featured uphill burnout areas. (Photo Courtesy Fred Simmons)

Southeastern International Dragway underwent a number of huge changes in its later years, after being shortened to a eighth mile. The complete concrete racing surface gave the track a major facelift, and it's still in great shape. Unfort nately, racing on this property is no longer an option.

SMITHVILLE DRAG STRIP

Although northern Georgia and northern Alabama had plenty of drag strips, venturing north of Chattanooga gave racers more choices. Northwest of the city was Smithville Drag Strip, located close to the downtown area of Smithville. It was just off Miller Road, less than 2 miles away from downtown. At the time, the track was quite popular with the locals, although it didn't have as big a following as some of the other tracks in the region. It did, however, serve as the home track for legendary Super Stock racer Charlie Lee, who campaigned a race-winning Chevy II for quite some time.

The track never turned into a major attraction, but it d provide a great place to race. Unfortunately, a tornado can through Smithville in April 1968, causing severe damage the drag strip. Among other damages, tin fencing that su rounded parts of the drag strip ended up scattered around t area. It was decided that the damage was too severe to co sider rebuilding the track, so the property owner stripped t drag strip of its goods and split the property into a housin subdivision. The old pavement is now Earl Avenue, which the main street through the neighborhood.

Distance from Chattanooga, 93 Miles
1960–1968

Current Status: ➤ **HOUSIN SUBDIVISIO**

LLOYD'S DRAG STRIP

There isn't much left of Lloyd's Drag Strip, aside from the actual strip of pavement. All other artifacts have been removed, as the property was developed into a small neighborhood. The uphill shutdown area is long gone, but the main part of the track is still visible.

Distance from Chattanooga, 99 Miles
1962–Late 1960s

Current Status: ➤ **ABANDONED**

With a name like Lloyd's Drag Strip, you might be able to guess the guy's name who started it all. Lloyd Young built the track in the mountainous town of Blairsville, Georgia. The location of the track was convenient for the mountain men of Georgia and North Carolina, but its backwoods location certainly kept it from growing into a big-time track.

The drag strip opened in late 1962 and only featured a small concrete launch pad—the rest was packed dirt. Huge improvements for the next year of operation meant a fully paved racing surface, which measured 1,056 feet in length. At one-fifth mile (sometimes referred to as two-tenths) the track was different than most Chattanooga-area tracks at the time. Lloyd's had an uphill shutdown area, with no return road until you got closer to the finish line.

With no lights, the track always ran races during the afternoon, generally on Sunday. Early in its life, the track didn't have electronic timing systems either, but changed to a homemade timing system in the later years of operation. To run the timing system, a man sat at the finish line with a battery-powered telephone and flipped a switch when the car crossed the finish line. This switch turned on a light, which signaled someone in the timing booth to stop a hand-held stopwatch. The finish-line watchman then told who won via telephone.

As you can tell, Lloyd's Drag Strip wasn't exactly a high-tech facility, but it gave folks a place to race. Lloyd's never had scales, so class structure was a bit different than at most tracks, which used the car's weight and cubic inches to determine its class ranking. Similar to its neighboring track, Double H Drag Strip in Blue Ridge, Georgia, Lloyd's offered Super Stock classes as well as the popular Cheatin' Four Barrel class, which had limited rules.

As the 1960s rolled on, the track didn't keep up with the times, and eventually closed. The pavement is still intact to this day, and serves as a private driveway to a few houses in the area.

Match Race

May 8

LLOYD'S DRAG STRIP

2 Best Out Of 3

Bill Bailey Driving Blairsville Motors Ford

VS.

Jerry Messer of Lincoln, Nebraska Driving A 1964, 426 Valiant

Plus

Promise Of 4 – 396 Chevys From Marietta

Gates Open 12:30   Races Start At 2:30

Adm $1.00

Race flyers in the 1960s were incredibly simple, but they were plastered all over Blairsville, Georgia, in order to get a big crowd to gather at Lloyd's Drag Strip. Match races were quite popular, but Lloyd's also had its share of Super Stock events. (Photo Courtesy Robert Turner)

HARRIMAN DRAG STRIP

Harriman Drag Strip didn't have the nicest facility in the region, but it offered weekly races that drew folks from all arou[nd] the area. It was never sanctioned, but Harriman delivered lots of excitement, thanks to a backwoods, outlaw atmosphe[re]. Super Stock races were always popular, as well as big match races like this one. (Photo Courtesy David Giles Collectio[n])

Distance from Chattanooga, 81 Miles
1956–1972

Current Status: ➤ **ABANDONE[D] OVERGROW[N]**

Located north of Chattanooga, this drag strip in Harriman, Tennessee, was a popular destination for local racers. Its location made it accessible to racers from Chattanooga and Knoxville as well as from Nashville and even Kentucky when a big purse was announced. Throughout its run from 1956 to 1972, it was never sanctioned, but held numerous events at its no-frills facility. Super Stock events were a big draw in the mid to late 1960s, and there were even

When Harriman Drag Strip closed in 1972, it wasn't kept clean, so trees took over the property and completely hid the remains of the track. Now that it has been sitting vacant for more than forty years, small portions of pavement are all that remain.

a few Pro Stock match races held at Harriman during its la[st] couple years of operation.

The landscape would be considered odd these days, [as] the drag strip was constructed very close to the Emory Riv[er]. So close, in fact, that a stuck throttle or brake failure cou[ld] potentially send you into the water. The flat ground near t[he] river was one of the only options for a drag strip in the hil[ly] town of Harriman, so the lake lot turned out to make a gre[at] track. Harriman was always known for its roug[h] neck qualities, as it was a fair distance off the beate[n] path, and a general lack of rules made for some ho[s]tile situations.

Like many Southern tracks, it only survived [a] few years after safety concerns caused a major ripp[le] effect throughout the industry. With no guardra[il] and little-to-no safety precautions, Harriman Dr[ag] Strip was a typical outlaw track of the time.

The track went through several ownersh[ip] changes during its existence, but when it shut dow[n] that was it—no more drag strip. The proper[ty] wasn't kept up after the closing of the track, so yo[u] can imagine what forty years of neglect can do [to] a place. Small patches of pavement remain, but th[e] rest of the track has been reclaimed by the earth.

GREEN VALLEY RACEWAY DRAG STRIP

reen Valley continued to be a great place to race until the 1980s when it was shut down. It was successfully revived, nd continued until 1997. The remains of the track are now used as a parking area for Green Valley Speedway, the neighboring dirt track that continues to have a great following. (Photo Courtesy Wayne Holland)

Distance from Chattanooga, 99 Miles
1959-1997

Current Status: ➤ **PARKING FOR DIRT TRACK**

While it may not have the legendary status of the well-known Green Valley Raceway in Texas, this "other" Green Valley Drag Strip has a legendary status in the opinions of its former racers. It was the go-to track for quite some time, for Chattanooga racers.

Located in Glencoe, Alabama, Green Valley Drag Strip was built in 1959 and was originally a full quarter-mile track. When it was opened, the track had four lessees who each had a stake in the property and business, but its glory days were during Milton Henson's management. Woodrow (Woody) Miller owned the property throughout all of the different lessees and track managers that cycled through.

Milton began managing the track in 1960, promoting all sorts of events including a great number of Super Stock meets as well as countless match races with folks such as Don Garlits and Tommy Ivo. During the first decade of his management, Green Valley was unsanctioned but used the NHRA's rules. Later, the IHRA sanctioned the track and held points races, which brought in a lot of business.

In 1977, Green Valley was shortened to an eighth mile, following the trend among many of its neighboring tracks due to safety concerns. Green Valley closed the drag strip in 1994, but reopened a couple years later, only to close again for good in 1997.

On the same piece of property as the drag strip was a clay dirt oval track, which drew thousands of spectators on a regu-

lar basis. Then, in 1963, a motorcycle flat track was built and sanctioned by the American Motorcycle Association. Currently, the dirt track still exists, while a smaller oval is used for go-kart racing.

The drag strip sits vacant. The retired strip is generally used for parking, and no longer has a tower or other buildings. As of this writing, there are no plans to revitalize the drag strip.

If you're familiar with the "big" Green Valley Raceway Drag Strip in Texas, then you might notice a theme with the checkered timing tower. Although the Glencoe, Alabama–based Green Valley had no affiliation with the other one, it served as a great destination for big-time races in the area. (Photo Courtesy Larry Rose Collection)

DRAG CITY

Drag City was located in Ringgold, Georgia, which was also the home of Brainerd Optimist Drag Strip. The two tracks generally worked in harmony and had great events in the 1960s, but Drag City closed in 1967. It then reopened and continued operation until 1984, when it closed permanently. (Photo Courtesy Bob Snyder)

Distance from Chattanooga, 19 Miles
1960–1984

Current Status: ➤ **ABANDONE**

One of the closest drag strips to Chattanooga was Drag City, located in Ringgold, Georgia. You may remember that Ringgold had another drag strip in this same time frame (Brainerd Optimist Drag Strip, page 160), but both tracks operated simultaneously without any major problems.

Drag City opened in the early 1960s and served as a great home for Gassers and Stock class racers. Drag City was a fifth-mile track (1,056 feet) even when other local tracks were running quarter-mile races.

The timing and light system was far from sophisticated, utilizing an old traffic light as the Christmas tree for several years. Even when the lights were upgraded to a proper five-amber Chrondek tree, the old traffic light remained in place.

As for the landscape, Drag City was in a fairly flat part of town, just off Highway 41, but a steep elevation came on the return road. A sharp right-hand turn at the end of the track sent racers into an uphill, single-lane return road that circled back around to the unpaved pits.

Funny Car legend Shirl Greer served as track manager, giving him a great place to test his creations. His involvement with the track also helped when it came to promoting big events. His Funny Car brethren visited the track many times, especially in the 1970s. As soon as the IHRA came onto the scene as a legitimate governing body, Drag City picked up sanctioning from that organization.

By 1984, the track had reached the end of its life cycle, an was stripped of all its guardrails, buildings, and timing equip ment. The property was subsequently sold to a church, whic quickly realized that the land was susceptible to floodin, They couldn't build without a lot of preliminary excavatin work. At the time of printing, the 38-acre piece of propert was for sale with an asking price of only $275,000.

The heyday of Drag City was under the managemer of Funny Car legend, Shirl Greer. His connections gav the track an advantage, as he could organize Funny Ca meets to bring in big crowds. The track was later know as Ringgold Dragway, and was managed by Chuck Heath (Photo Courtesy Bob Snyder)

One of the most interesting abandoned race tracks in the Chattanooga area is Loudon Raceway, near Knoxville. The track had a good following of racers, but closed before the TVA flooded the land during the controversial Tellico Dam project in 1979. The silos were part of the farmland where the track had been built.

Distance from Chattanooga, 96 Miles
1960–1970s

Current Status: ➤
UNDERWATER

Loudon Raceway was another hometown Southern track essentially in the middle of nowhere. To get to the track, you took an old farm road that cut through a few hundred acres of farmland. It was a scenic setting, which was normal for the area, but it didn't lend itself well to huge events, or the potential for growth in the area. The track was a decent haul from the Chattanooga area, and got a great mix of racers from the Knoxville, Tennessee, area as well. The town of Loudon was rather small, but the drag strip drew folks from all around in its heyday.

Although the track closed in the 1970s, the remains might still be around to this day if not for one strange occurrence. The property of Loudon Raceway is now completely under-water, thanks to the intentional flooding of the area in 1979. The Tennessee Valley Authority (TVA) built the Tellico Dam as one of its many power sources, but an opposition uproar was heard when an endangered fish was discovered in this section of the Little Tennessee River. Many of the Snail Darters were transported to the nearby Hiwassee River, but the drag strip did not survive.

Although several holdouts remained in their houses until the final few days of dry land, the area was indeed flooded on November 29, 1979, and Loudon Raceway was never seen again. However, you can still see a couple of silos poking up out of the water, reminders of the farmland that the drag strip was built upon.

The tracks that managed to survive through the toughest times of drag racing history still have a tough row to hoe, because politics, safety, and the economy still determine the livelihood of most tracks. Large or small, drag strip owners are sitting on pins and needles because of all the rules and regulations required to do business, while also fighting a slump in the economy and the ongoing evolution of the cars. The fact that the NHRA fuel classes shortened the racing distance to 1,000 feet is enough to show that the history of the sport doesn't hold a candle to the safety of the drivers and fans. Racing organizations, track owners, and racers will do whatever it takes to keep the sport going, even if it means doing away with standard quarter-mile racing. Eighth-mile racing has become popular because it's the only accessible track for many racers, so they just have to deal with it; the same goes for those who are forced to race 1,000 feet instead of the full 1,320.

Modern-day drag strips, regardless of whether they are historic or brand-new facilities, face the same challenges that most tracks have faced over the years. Even state-of-the-art tracks can be forced to close if enough people are involved with the complaints or surrounding property development.

Since the turn of the century, many tracks have bitten the dust and the coming years aren't looking any better for the sport. Drag cars aren't exactly "green" so they definitely don't sit well with environmentalists, who have an alarming amount of pull in the automotive world. Luckily, organizations such as the Specialty Equipment Market Association (SEMA) go to bat for the automotive aftermarket industry and have been quite successful in keeping the hot rod and

Packed stands and crowded staging lanes didn't affect the decision to close Kansas City International Raceway (KCIR), leaving hundreds of racers without a home track. It was sanctioned by the NHRA and held many big events. It was also one of the stops on *Hot Rod* magazine's Drag Week event on more than one occasion. (Photo Courtesy Kyle Loftis)

rag racing community on good terms with government regulations.

Regardless of SEMA's efforts, tracks are closing at a shocking rate. At the end of 2011, a number of tracks faced certain death, while others closed temporarily and returned under new ownership or management. One of them was Tulsa Raceway Park, but a last-minute agreement from Todd Martin and Keith Haney resulted in the formation of T&K Management Group, which promised to keep Tulsa Raceway Park alive for several more years.

Another track in turmoil was in Los Angeles, Irwindale Raceway, which filed for bankruptcy in early 2012. A change of hands is always touchy with noise ordinances, which are particularly strict in Southern California, but it was possible to continue under different ownership.

Auto Club Dragway in Fontana, California, was not so lucky. In early 2012, its website read, "A Superior Court has suspended operation of the Auto Club Dragway." The statement continued, "The suspension results from a successful challenge of a San Bernardino County sound standard by a group of concerned residents." In other words, the track was forced to close because of noise complaints.

Sunshine Drag Strip, Lakeland Drag Strip, and Emerald Coast Dragway, all located in Florida, closed their gates temporarily during late 2011 and early 2012. However, ownership changes gave hope to many Florida racers who thought they would no longer have a place to race.

Several hundred racers in the Midwest didn't have that luxury, as the city of Kansas City struck a deal to buy their Kansas City International Raceway (KCIR), with plans to turn it into a park immediately. This drag racing facility had been in business since 1967. The longtime track underwent this unfortunate exchange in late 2011, and it has already been dismantled in preparation for the city park development. Even with a successful NHRA sanction, as well as great support from its racers the track couldn't fight the local government any longer. KCIR ran its final race on November 27, 2011.

On the Rebound

With hundreds of drag strips going out of business in the late 1970s and early 1980s, the push for a triumphant comeback was inevitable. Drag racers wanted a safe place to race, and many of them got together hoping to reopen some of the tracks had that closed due to the bad economy. And while the effort was tremendous, most abandoned drag strips had little-to-no option for reopening, regardless of the number of improvements to the facility.

In most cases, it wasn't a matter of the track condition—it was the local government that simply didn't want the complaints, or it came down to the property being sold to a developer who had no interest in drag racing. Many drag strips were destroyed in favor of a park, a housing subdivision, or an industrial park before a group could step in to revive the track.

A select few racers were lucky enough to succeed in bringing back their home track. In the 1980s, several tracks reopened after only a couple years of closure, but the tracks included in this list never really looked like they were truly abandoned.

When it comes to reviving an abandoned drag strip, especially a track that has been vacant for more than a few years,

KCIR didn't have any revolutionary equipment or a high-tech tower, but it was a great track that worked nicely for a wide range of cars. Unfortunately, politics got in the way of drag racing, so the track was bought by the city of Kansas City in late 2011, with plans to build a new city park immediately. (Photo Courtesy Kyle Loftis)

Tracks such as Drag City in Ringgold, Georgia, had several instances of closures and re-openings. Throughout the ownership and management changes, it certainly didn't have a stable crew but survived until 1984. Drag City was home to the Southeastern Super Stock Championship race, as well as several Funny Car meets. (Photo Courtesy Bob Snyder)

it's no simple task. Lots of paperwork is involved and if the property changed ownership during the down time, there isn't much hope unless the facility is not under the firm grasp of noise and other strict ordinances. A few tracks have been thoughtfully revived after sitting vacant for several years, so there's something to be said about the perseverance of drag racers.

There aren't very many tracks that made it out of abandonment, especially in areas where real estate values far surpassed the value of a racing facility. That's why the success stories with tracks such as 75-80 Dragway in Monrovia, Maryland, are so great. The track opened in 1960, had a successful run as one of the premier tracks on the East Coast, and was known specifically for its "Run What Ya Brung" heads-up events. A lack of maintenance caused a continuous drop in attendance, until it all came crumbling down in 2005, when the track finally closed its doors.

And while most folks thought they'd never have another world-renowned chili dog from Monrovia, Maryland's 75-80 Dragway, rumors floated around the Internet about new activity at the track. Some doubted the reality of the track reopening, but it was happening—75-80 was being reborn, thanks to a few fresh faces. Roy Stanley, along with his son, Kevin, and daughter, Lisa Stanley-Willis, reached an agreement with property owner Bill Wilcom to manage the track. Wilcom still served as a consultant, but left the big decisions to the Stanley family.

During the down time, the track had really gone downhill, but the Stanley family did a lot to bring it back to life. New roofs for the buildings, new concrete barriers to replace the steel guardrails, and a thorough cleanup did wonders to wake up the sleepy drag strip. October 2009 was the grand reopening of 75-80 Dragway and it has been one of the biggest success stories for abandoned track revival.

Another notable track that has seen a major rejuvenatic is Lassiter Mountain Dragway in Mount Olive, Alabama. was one of Alabama's first drag strips, opening its doors i 1958, and it was certainly one of the most recognizable track in the country, with its carved-out racing surface and hug vertical rock walls on both sides of the track. Spectators ha an interesting view of the racing action, and the cliffs mea that guardrails were not necessary to protect the crowd. Th track saw lots of success over the years, but a laundry list c upgrades was necessary to keep it alive. Lassiter Mountai which also operated as Birmingham Dragway, closed in 200 and the property sat vacant for a few years, until new owne completely renovated it and reopened in 2010. The cliffs ar gone, new concrete guard walls are in place, and the tower ha been completely rebuilt.

Onondaga Dragway in Michigan is yet another track th sat abandoned, and gets the award for most years in abandor ment. It sat unused from its closure 1978 until 2009, when group of racers held a reunion event on the old track. Th involvement sparked an interest in reviving the track, an thousands of dollars and countless hours resulted in a grea looking race track. The racers installed new guardrails an completely revamped the racing surface, only to be held up b local politics. At the time of print, the track had been comple for more than a year, but had not seen its first official day c use. However, that's not to say it hasn't seen a few passes b racers such as Jeff Cook, who devoted lots of time and mone to reviving the historic Michigan track.

Without question, there are lots of tracks that could b revived if the opportunity presented itself. Generally, the rac ing surface can be redone, but that's the easiest part of th equation. It's always the final details that give the most troubl and they involve paperwork to obtain proper insurance, ord nances, and regulations. Even though many drag strips cor tinue to sit in an abandoned state, it isn't for the lack of tryin

Maryland had several great drag strips in the 1960s, including 75-80 Dragway. It was home to a heads-up event known as "Run What Ya Brung" and still has the event to this day. In the 1960s, the event was an outlaw Super Stock meet, and today, it's based on outlaw street cars. (Photo Courtesy John Durand)

When 75-80 Dragway reopened in 2009, it required coun less hours of labor to refurbish the racing surface and giv all of the buildings a thorough restoration. The track cor tinues to prosper, holding its popular "Run What Ya Brung heads-up events on a regular basis, along with a regula IHRA racing program. (Photo Courtesy Matt Ebaugh)

Although it received thousands of dollars worth of renovations, Onondaga Dragway patiently awaits the paperwork necessary to open for business. Jeff Cook and several other dedicated racers began using the track privately in 2009, and began the renovations shortly thereafter. Local politics are the main reason for the hold up. (Photo Courtesy Jeff Cook)

undreds of tracks across the country face certain death at the end f each year's season. Whether it's due to ownership changes, local overnment, or the ailing economy, drag strips struggle to stay alive. these tracks lose the support of their racers, it won't take long for ne track owners to pull the plug.

Mount Olive, Alabama, resident and long-time racer Randall Shew played a big part in the revival of Lassiter Mountain Dragway. Here, he stands in front of the track, which underwent a major renovation prior to its grand re-opening in 2010. Track owners Jay Bostic and Donald Phillips made great improvements to the facility. (Photo Courtesy *The North Jefferson News*)

Vhen 75-80 Dragway closed in 2005, it already looked abandoned. The lack of attention had gotten the best of the rack, but a new management team gave it major improvements in preparation for a huge rebound. Despite the track's oor condition, its final event in 2005 drew an enormous crowd. (Photo Courtesy Matt Ebaugh)

INDEX

Additional books that may interest you...

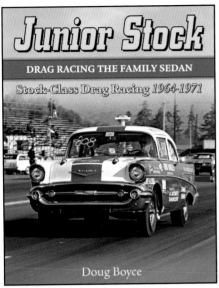
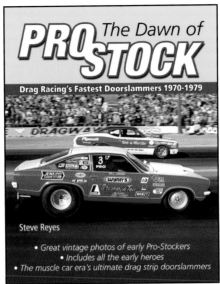
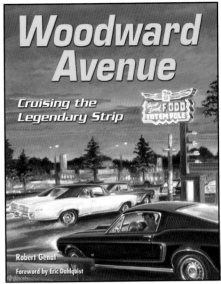
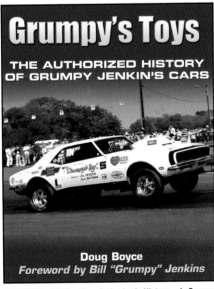